Successful
Big Game Hunting

SECRETS OF A BIG GAME HUNTER-GUIDE

By Duncan Gilchrist

Published in the United States of America

Successful Big Game Hunting

Secrets of a Big Game Hunter-Guide

By Duncan Gilchrist

Copyright 1987 by Duncan Gilchrist

ISBN 0-912299-27-4 (Hardcover)
ISBN 0-912299-28-2 (Softcover)

Stoneydale Press Publishing Co.
205 Main Street — Drawer B
Stevensville, Montana 59870
Phone: 406-777-2729

Dedication

I would like to dedicate this book to the man who I feel has done more to promote quality hunting and good sportsmanship than another other person in the United States. Throughout his life he has always found time to help others in need of advice, to fight for better game management, to be involved in any and all ways possible to enhance the sport of big game hunting, with no thoughts of reward. He has done all this without being on an ego trip. He is a sportsman among sportsmen. Thank you Jack Atcheson Sr.

Table of Contents

COVER PHOTO

The photo on the front cover of this book depicts author Duncan Gilchrist with a fine mule deer buck taken on a hunting trip to the Missouri Breaks of central Montana. The picture was taken by his son, Stuart.

Quebec whitetail. Photo by Jim Bush.

Introduction

After having written several books covering diversified hunting topics with titles including: *Trophy Rams Of The Brooks Range, Hunting The Rocky Mountain Goat, On Bears And Bear Hunting, Journal Of A High Country Hunter* and *The Big Game Hunter's and Fishermen's Complete Guide To The Field Care Of Trophies*, literally hundreds of readers have written or called. Some want advice, others wish to criticize and some express thoughts on what they would like to read. Most readers of hunting literature definitely want to learn new techniques, find out where to go to get the best results, and learn what equipment they should purchase and use.

For the past several years I have been keeping notes on what material appears to be in the greatest demand by the reading public. In this book, I have attempted to bring to the hunter information which should assist him in being a more successful big game hunter, without being too repetitious of other authors.

Hopefully the material within these pages will help all big game hunters, but I feel that the do-it-yourself hunter will profit the most, as most of my experiences have been as a guide and self-taught sportsman; all on a limited budget. Never will I claim that my system is the only correct method for I truly believe that there is generally more than one way to achieve success. My methods work and you won't stray too far by using them.

Author packing out a trophy mule deer rack.

Chapter One

SOME THOUGHTS ON RIFLE MARKSMANSHIP FOR THE BIG GAME HUNTER

The hunter's ability with his rifle can mean the difference between success and failure. Many a man has spent the better part of a lifetime in hope of downing a particular species, or maybe an usually large trophy, only to miss when the moment of opportunity arrived. It matters little if the miss can be blamed on faulty equipment, a jerked trigger or just plain inability.

I can find no logic in spending thousands of dollars on that hunt of a lifetime, only to use inadequate shooting equipment, or to be unable to hit because of lack of practice, or knowledge of basic shooting practices and ballistics.

I am constantly amazed at the small number of persons who understand what happens to the bullet once it leaves the barrel. I don't claim to know it all, or to be a top marksman. While in college I didn't shoot well enough to make the small bore rifle team, but was so dedicated to the sport that I was named the manager. In this chapter I plan to pass on what I have learned over the years. This information will hopefully make you a more successful hunter.

One late fall day about two decades ago, I fired nearly a box of shells at a herd of mountain goats without scoring a hit. After each miss I aimed higher. In my mind they were beyond the practical range of my 264. In desperation I finally fired a shot holding dead on. To my amazement I scored a hit. I never forgot this lesson. There are a large number of flat shooting calibers on the market and yet a great many hunters refuse to accept their benefits. After having asked a client, "How is your rifle sighted in?" His response has frequently been, "Why right on at a 100 yards," or maybe "An inch high at a 100 " What a total waste of a flat trajectory.

From a Winchester-Western range table you can find that a 270 Winchester loaded with 130 grainSpitzer softpoints and sighted in to be dead on at 100 yards, will be 10.5 inches low at 300 yards, 24.5 below at 400 and 45 1/2 inches low at 500 yards. Sight in to be 3.5 inches high at 100 and you will be 4.4 high at 200, on at 300, 10.5 low at 400 and 28 inches low at 500 yards. If you are shooting at deer-size animals with an average body width of 18 inches, and you aim half way up, you will hit out to about 270 yards, if sighted to be on at a hundred. If your scope is adjusted so you are 3 1/2 high at 100 and still hold the same you will hit out to at least 370 yards; a full 100 yard difference. So what if you are a bit high at 100, and 200. It will not cause you to miss a big game animal. In my experience, any time a hunter has to start holding over he will probably miss.

As a practical matter, I sight all my rifles, except the heavies, to hit 3 inches high at 100. My 270 is loaded with 130 grain Sierra Boattails, backed with 57.5 grains of H-205, with an instrumental velocity in my barrel of 3192 f.p.s. It hits as follows: 3 inches high at 100 yards, 4 high at 200, on at 275, 10 low at 400 and about 27 low at 500 yards. Use any flat trajectory rifle and you will have about the same figures. Don't believe it? Listen to these figures taken right from the tables. An 80 grain bullet leaving the barrel at 3500, in a 243, and sighted in to be 3 inches high at 100, will be 26.5 low at 500. Only a half inch difference from the 270. The same table shows that even the hot 7mm mag with 150 grain bullets, and sighted in the same will arrive also 26.5 low at 500. The Weatherby series shoots a mite flatter to 500 but not by much.

I have found that in any given rifle a heavier longer bullet, because of its better ballistic shape, will arrive at 500 yards as flat as, or almost so, as a lighter projectile. After over a quarter century, of long range shooting, I am convinced that light bullets aren't the way to go for the long range big game hunter. This statement needs to be tempered, however, for I am assuming the shooter is using a bullet with an ideal ballistic shape for velocity retention. As an extreme example, round-nosed projectiles lose their speed much faster than Spitzer bullets.

When I was in my early twenties and an ardent reader of Jack O'Connor, he advised that that the long range shooter should never hold over on his first shot. The distance might not be as far as you think. He further stated that low shots are much easier to spot than high ones. If I have ever learned one thing about hunting through the written word it has been the above.

O'Connor was always an advocate of sighting in to be 3 inches high at 100 yards, to maximize your rifle's hitting potential, as far out as possible. Bob Hagel has carried the theory of long range shooting even further in his excellent book *Game Loads and Practical Ballistics For The American Hunter*. He has devised many tables showing bullet drop at various

Author's son, Brian, with a styrafoam pellet-filled pillow for open-country antelope and deer hunting.

ranges with a multitude of combinations of cartridges, bullets and powder. The last column shows the theoretical maximum vital hit distance on big game animals, of various species, with a center hold. Of course he has assumed a body width. As an example, one table shows that a 6mm Rem with a 95 grain Nosler backed with 47 grains of 4350 capable of making a vital hit on a deer, with a center hold to 340 yards. A great many hunters on a 340-yard shot would be needlessly holding over the back and probably miss. I think all open country big game hunters should own a copy of Hagel's book.

After 400 yards when reduced velocity begins to dominate, and bullet drop becomes more pronounced, the hunter should either refrain from firing, or learn the fine points of long range shooting.

The high country of Alaska provided lots of opportunities at long range big game shooting, but I did not refine my methods until moving to Montana. After Russ Moody and I began to hunt antelope together, we decided to improve our techniques in order to increase the percentage of way-out-yonder hits. Several friends hunting pronghorns with us had difficulty in hitting past 200 yards. We thought that a rest should certainly help, so we began carrying a sleeping bag in a stuff sack. The bag assisted in holding but it was too unhandy to tote. We soon made pillow shaped rests filled with foam pellets. Did they work? To this day I habitually carry my rest when it is at all feasible. It has made the difference between success and failure for many of my clients. With it even a so-so shooter has a reasonable chance of hitting on fairly long shots. My son Brian killed his first four big game animals with four shots with the help of a pillow rest.

Now that we had a method for holding the rifle steady we needed to know where to aim. One day after a series of long range misses on pronghorn bucks, I asked Russ what he thought about buying a rangefinder. My buddy appeared surprised that I didn't know that a duplex reticle could be used as a rangefinder. He was soon explaining the method. "The tips of the posts subtend a known distance at a hundred yards, usually somewhere between 16 and 20 inches. The distance can be found in the manufacturer's specifications, or you can set up a measuring stick at a known hundred yards. An antelope buck's body is about 16 inches in thickness and a muley's is 18 to 20 inches. As we are antelope hunting, let's use this animal as an example. My Leupold 4X duplex subtends 16 inches at 100 yards from post tip to post tip. If the animal's body fits exactly between the tips, then he is 100 yards away. If he fits between the post tip and the intersection of the crosshairs in the center of the scope, then he is 200 yards. If the body appears half as thick as the distance from the crosshair intersection and a post tip, then the distance is 400 yards. Past this point there is a bit of guesswork needed, but it will certainly place you in the ball park. You can tell if holdover is needed at the very least. So far our range estimation has been so bad that we have been aiming high when we shouldn't and not holding over when we ought to."

Once the method was adopted, the percentage of long range hits increased dramatically. After every kill I try to pace the distance to the animal. I have checked my pace against known distances many times and can consistently come within 95 percent of the true distance. I have paced and recorded the range to over two-thirds of the animals we have killed during the past decade. That first fall, Russ collected his buck at a paced 507 yards while mine was at 450.

This past season, each of my sons and I had second antelope tags, good for does only. My first opportunity was at a female antelope that appeared slightly smaller than half the distance between the post and intersection of the crosshairs, which would indicate over 400 yards. As the 130 grain Sierra Boattail, powered by 57.5 grains of H-205 in my 270 is about 10 inches low at that range, I held for the top of the back. She took off in a mad 25-yard run then fell to the ground. Pacing showed I had made a 412 yard hit. As this was my first shot of the fall I felt smug. I didn't shoot again until the next day when I saw an unusually large pronghorn buck standing on the next butte. My duplex showed the animal to be 600 yards away. I don't normally fire shots at that range, but since there is little chance of losing a wounded antelope I decided to try. I held an estimated three feet over. Was I amazed when I saw his rear end kick. I didn't kill him outright, but he was hurt bad enough that I was able to walk up to him within a few yards. I paced the distance twice and the range was calculated as 588 yards, the longest killing hit of my life. My trophy proved to have heavy 15 1/8 horns and a 5 1/4 inch prong. I am certain that I would never have made this kill without my portable rest and my impromptu rangefinder.

Working as an outfitter and guide for many years, I have never ceased to be amazed at how few clients rifles are sighted in. Two years ago at Jim Keeline's Icy Bay, Alaska, camp, I accompanied all clients to the bench. Out of about a dozen hunters, only one didn't need a scope adjustment.

When I visit the local range, all manner of shooters are firing from the bench, but seldom do I see anyone shooting offhand, kneeling, sitting or prone. In the world of big game hunting, how often does one get to shoot from a rest. Some, like antelope hunters, may get to fire from a rest fairly often, but it is not as practical a shooting position as some of the others. Over the years, I have noticed that clients from the East tend to shoot offhand. I suppose this comes about as most of their hunting is at running whitetails at close range. Offhand is the least accurate position of all, so should only be used as a last resort.

The prone position is almost as accurate as shooting from a rest, but in most environments it can seldom be used for once the hunter is laying on the ground low vegetation will usually obscure the target. Prone can be often used to advantage when shooting in the high alpine, where most plants are only a couple of inches high. Most pronghorn habitats are shy on high vegetation also, so prone can be used. When we are hunting on the open plains of eastern Montana, we carry a pillow filled with styrafoam pellets. Using a rest combined with firing from the prone position even relatively poor, or inexperienced shooters, are able to make remarkable hits.

I start my sons big game hunting by shooting from a pillow rest. My youngest boy, Brian, went on his first hunt when he was 12. He was far from ready, as he was not shooting well at all. Without the rest, the barn door would have been safe. The first shot he ever fired at a big game animal was at an antelope, which he killed at 250 paced yards. Later in the day, he dropped a mule deer at 75 paced yards with his second shot. This past fall it was Brian's second season in the field. He was still not shooting well, but better than he had at 12. His first shot of the year and his third of his life was at a ewe bighorn which dropped at the shot at 180 yards. His next was at an antelope at 154 yards; an instant kill. Brian collected two more big game animals in 1985, but he finally did a bit of missing. I truly think my son's record of killing four animals with four shots, even though he could be a considered a poor shot, goes to show what an aid a rest can be. In 1986, he fired three shots and downed two antelope and a deer.

In the mountains one is often able to shoot from a rock ledge or boulder. When completing my final stalk in the high country, I plan my approach to take me from rest to rest. I have always felt that it is best to take a long shot from a solid position, than a closer shot at a fleeing animal fired offhand, or from an insecure position.

Next to using a rest, the most practical shooting position is sitting, with or without a sling. Properly executed it is nearly as steady as prone, with the added advantage that the rifle barrel is high enough above the ground to allow the shooter to see over any intervening vegetation. Successful shooters use a variety of variations of this position. The key is to never place the elbows on the knees. One will slide on the other causing a wobble, which results in a position that isn't much better than shooting offhand.

The sitting position can be assumed in a wide variety of terrains from flat timberlands to steep mountain slopes. Over the years, I have trained myself to drop instantly into sitting, ready for action. I have killed about 60 percent of my larger animals from this position.

To assume the normal sitting posture, the shooter faces away from his target at about a 40 degree angle. He then leans forward placing the upper arm, above the elbow, on the inside of the knees. The heels should be flat on the ground and I have found when shooting on steep slopes it helps considerably to dig one's heels into the dirt.

When the country is flat enough to allow the method, I use the crosslegged sitting position. I hook my right ankle around my left and drop instantly onto my butt. The elbows are hooked into the fleshy area just above the inside of the knees. I have found the position to be exceedingly fast and accurate. A good shooter should be able to keep all shots in 10 inches at 300 yards.

Accuracy can be further improved by the proper use of a sling. If you are using the military type, it can be adjusted to allow the upper left arm to be placed in a loop, creating a steadying tension between the rifle and the shooter's shoulder. When properly adjusted, a sling is 33 to 36 inches long depending upon the distance between the sling swivels. The sling is adjusted by changing the location of the hooks where they attach to the holes. The loop needs to be adjusted just right, for if it is too tight one can hardly use it and if too loose the sling is of little benefit. You will probably have to make several adjustments before a proper fit is achieved. The loop is correct when it takes pressure from your right hand to place the rifle's buttplate to your shoulder. So adjusted, this is perfect for target shooting, but it should be a little looser for hunting. Once set correctly, I permanently secure the sling with a shoelace.

To use a sling in the sitting position, first hold the rifle upwards giving the loop a quarter turn to the left. Place the left arm through the loop as far as you can. Tighten the keepers until the loop is secure. Bring the left hand around to the left of the sling and on up to the forward swivel. With the right hand bring the buttplate to the shoulder. If you learn to shoot in this manner, you will be amazed at the accuracy you achieve.

Kneeling is one of the standard positions in an NRA course, but I have found little use for it in hunting. It gives no advantages over sitting and yet is not nearly as accurate.

I have seen a few hunters that gain accuracy by resting the fore-end of their rifle along a stick. Some use a manufactured shooting stick, while others pick up whatever is handy in the field.

Much has been placed in print about uphill and downhill shooting. All kinds of magic formulas are given about holding over, or under, or whatever. It is amazing how my clients have messed up long shots on up or down steep slopes. There is only one fact that needs to be remembered: GRAVITY. All falling objects drop the same distance over a given period of time. What does this mean to you and your rifle bullet? ONLY HORIZONTAL DISTANCE COUNTS. If your target is 500 slope yards away, but only 350 yards horizontal distance, take the shot as though it was 350 yards. It makes no difference if it is uphill or downhill. Most inexperienced hunters miss these long shots as they hold over. I'll bet for every missed shot being low there are a dozen over the animal. ONLY HORIZONTAL DISTANCE COUNTS.

I think a few thoughts on stock material are worthy of note. Most everyone agrees that wood is the most pleasing material aesthetically from which to build a rifle stock. For years, hunters in the harsher environments of the world have been seeking something better. Stocks of alternating laminations of walnut and maple have been on the market for two decades, or better. One will minimize stock warping and bullet impact

Author ready to fire at a buck from the sitting position.

Author getting ready to shoot from the sitting position.

changes. More recently, synthetic stock materials have appeared on the market. I have been using my Brown Precision fibreglass stock for a decade with superb results. Even under the most severe conditions, I have made no sight changes, except for one, which was due to a scope malfunction.

Brown Precision, the innovator of the synthetic stock, claims that rifle weight can be reduced 1 1/2 pounds by the use of one of their stocks, along with the advantage of absolute stability. Most shooters say that glass stocks look terrible. They are correct. There is no beauty in the synthetic stock. Brown's catalog has this to say: "Unlike wood stocks, fibreglass is not affected by humidity, rain and extreme temperature variations, thus maintaining its bedding and most important its point of impact. Lighter and stronger than wood, resistant to brush damage, breakage and scabbard wear, and absolutely stable, they eliminate a source of disappointment and frustration." Brown says that the addition of graphite to the fore-end assures the stiffest, toughest stock available.

Another new synthetic is Kelvar. It is claimed to be a super strong lightweight material which produces a stock up to 1/4-pound lighter than fibreglass. The problem with Kelvar is that it is hard to work and it is expensive.

The synthetic stock is here to stay and several custom firms are producing rifles that combine the synthetic stock with totally rust free barrels and actions. Two of note are located in Montana — Gentrys in Bozeman and Mark Wright of Livingston. The synthetic stock is even beginning to appear in the mass manufactured rifle field such as by Weatherby.

Alpha Arms of Dallas, Texas, is using another system to gain stability by impregnating wood with resin. They claim complete stability without excessive weight. Maybe one can have stability and beauty too?

I am sold on the synthetic stock. I prefer to look at a fine trophy on the wall rather than a fancy piece of wood that was the cause of a missed shot.

Chapter Two

SOME THOUGHTS ON GEAR FOR THE BIG GAME HUNTER

I make no claim of knowing it all, but after a quarter century of hunting in the WORLD'S game fields I have formed some definite thoughts on equipment and its use. I hope that the information in this chapter will help you, and maybe save you a few wasted dollars by avoiding the purchase of improper equipment.

When I first began big game hunting there did not seem to be much variety in equipment available for the hunter. In the 1970's the market became flooded with goodies: boots, tents, food stuffs, stoves, packs and a never-ending array of new products. Why all these new items I cannot say. During that era nearly every hitchhiker one would see along the highway would be armed with Vibram soled boots, a lightweight sleeping bag and an ultra-light packframe. Seriously, I can't believe that all those souls were taking to the high country. I think that it was a fad just like camo clothing is in the mid-80's. Today, we the serious backpacking hunters are fortunate, as the grocery store shelves have become stocked with an ever-expanding assortment of lightweight foods.

Most beginning backpackers carry too much. It is amazing how little one really needs. I know, I too once carried the closet!

Knives

Today our sporting good stores and catalogs are filled with a wide assortment of cutlery. It is easy to fall under the spell of a $100 knife, with steel so hard that it is guaranteed to cut through the thigh bones of six elk and four moose without sharpening. What do I use for a knife? My basic is

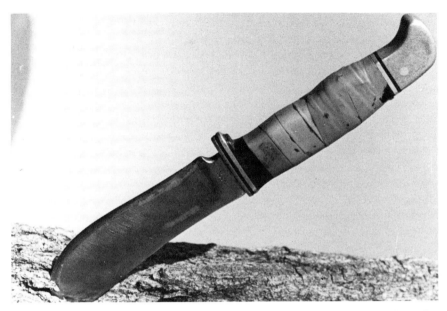

The author has owned and used this Buck fleshing knife for over 30 years. The yellow and blue tape on the handle makes the knife easier to find if mislaid in the field.

an Old Timer, three-bladed, pocket knife. It is easy to carry and will do the job. It fills 90 percent of my hunting needs. I have completely butchered animals as large as moose, and it has skinned Alaskan brown bear. It may not be perfect, but it will do.

I have used many other knives, and I regularly use specialty blades. For fleshing I use a Buck Skinner, a Gerber Flayer, a Forschner, a Green River or an Eskimo ulu. All work on the principle of a lot of cutting with each stroke of the blade. The Buck and the Gerber are very hard, making sharpening a tedious process. A Buck knife, as it is bought, has an edge much too thick to be of any use to the hunter. One must thin the knife to a practical, thinner angle. To thin the blade, I use a belt sander, being careful to stay away from the edge, which would draw the temper, making the knife worthless. CAREFUL! To finish the sharpening job, I use a diamond impregnated steel. I can maintain my Old Timer with but a few strokes of a steel or stone, while it may take several minutes to hone one of the harder blades to adequate sharpness. It should be apparent that I like knives of softer steel, while many hunters do insist that their blades be made from hard steel.

When backpacking I generally bone my meat, and have found that I can do a much neater job with a knife designed for boning. The one I use is a Forschner with a five inch blade that is a half inch wide. The steel is moderately hard, yet it is easy to sharpen. With it, I am able to quickly bone a complete animal, with a minimum of wasted meat. Often, I carry a large Old Timer pocket knife in a sheaf, which has a single four inch blade. I like this knife, as it is easy to maintain, and the blade has enough belly to make a fairly efficient fleshing tool.

You do not need a long blade to have a good hunting knife. Many years ago a client gave me a Gerber Big Hunter with a five inch blade. My wife uses it as a kitchen knife, as I can find no use for it in the field.

For sharpening purposes I use both stones and steels and have owned and used many types. Today, I am carrying an Eze-Lap, which is impregnated with diamonds. With it most cutting edges can be restored with a few strokes. Most people when they first acquire a sharpening steel, do not realize how little effort it takes to hone an edge. It is easy to wear away your blade with a steel.

Many hunters feel that a meat saw has to be carried in the field. They are handy for splitting briskets, removal of feet and head, but are not really needed. I have butchered dozens, if not hundreds, of big game animals

The author commonly uses many knives for hunting. From left to right: Old Timer Pocket knife, a single blade pocket knife, a boning blade and a fleshing knife.

with only a knife. Legs, skulls, and hams can be removed by cutting through the appropriate joints. When backpacking, a saw is nice for reducing a trophy skull to minimum size, but I generally leave the saw at home, and pack out the entire upper skull.

Photography Equipment

Most serious sportsmen treasure pictures of their trips. When in the mountains, we have the opportunity to photograph some of the most scenic areas in the world. Let there be no argument: the big 35mm single lens reflex cameras do the best job. When backpacking, I soon found my large reflex camera grew heavier and bulkier as the years passed. From 1969 through 1971, I doubt if I carried mine once while hunting. It was too much bother. When my home burned, I lost 99 percent of my photos. I think I mourned the loss of my photographs more than my trophies. I vowed to never be without a camera again, while in the field. I bought another single lens reflex and a cheap 110. The 110 would make it practical to always carry a camera in the field? I soon found that this small format did not produce quality pictures. Years later I purchased a Minolta 110 single lens reflex. It is compact, has a macro zoom lens, and is adjustable — but it too will not produce high quality photos. For snapshots it is great. I asked other serious hunters what they carried? Rick Furniss and Jack Atcheson both told me to buy a Rollei 35, which is a small 3 5/8 X 2 1/4 X 1 1/4 inch full frame 35, completely adjustable, and with a lens that folds into the body when not in use. I have been 100 percent satisfied with this camera. It is so small, that I am never without it. At the time of purchase it was the world's smallest full frame 35. Today, there are other 35's that are about as compact. The small Pentax is popular and it even has a built in strobe light.

To my carrying strap I have taped several empty 35mm film cans, in which to carry extra film. These containers are 100 percent waterproof, so I do not have to worry about damage to my film, and I am never without extra.

Don't get me wrong, I think all sportsmen should own and use a single lens reflex. With it one is able to to take extreme closeups, along with the ability to use a telephoto for wildlife shots. My Minolta XG 7 has an electronic film winder. With this rapid winder I can quickly shoot a series of wildlife shots, when the opportunity arises. I often photograph elk from my airplane, and with this camera over a dozen frames can be exposed in a single pass of the plane, instead of one or two without the winder; a nice feature. I also use a pair of Minolta SRT's. They are manual cameras, so can be relyed on being trouble free on all occasions, and I don't worry about dead batteries.

Today, most cameras have automatic metering systems, so we have become a generation of lazy photographers. We trust our cameras, but cameras do not think. If we are photographing a dead animal, it is the main subject, and the exposure should be calculated accordingly. Expose for the animal, which may require one or two f stops of additional light.

Some of the finest hunting photographs I have ever seen were black and whites owned by the famous Alaskan pioneer and guide, Harry Boyden, and were taken in the 30's. Today, we would laugh at the equipment used in those times, but they got results.

First Aid Kit

When hunting in the back country, the sportsman can ill afford any extra gear, but there are a few first aid items that I like to have along. Band Aids can save the day if you should be unlucky enough to develop a blister on the heel. More high country hunts have been ruined by blisters than any other cause. A Band Aid on my heel has made the difference between success and failure on more than one of my sheep or goat hunts. I also carry a small bottle of pain killer (Tylenol) for relief of headaches. Chapped lips are a common problem for those not used to the the wind. You should carry some sort of remedy for them. I like Carmex or bag balm. They are a bit messy, but either provides lasting relief and protection.

I used to think that hunters to the back country should carry antibiotics in case of a serious injury. My doctor, who is a hunter, always told me that infection in the field is a minor problem, compared to the damage one could do to a person, who is allergic to the stuff. I ignored his advice.

My son, Stuart, was accompanying me on an extended deer, antelope and turkey hunt to eastern Montana. He was suffering from an acute sore throat. I thought that he might have strepthroat, so started administering penicillin. The pills didn't help his throat, and he turned out to be allergic to penicillin, and his joints swelled up. Back home, it took several weeks for him to recover from the antibiotics I so foolishly had given him.

One other item I have carried for years is a couple of small surgical needles, with dental floss for thread. It is a gruesome thought that one would ever need to sew up a companion, but it might happen. It did occur to me, in 1977 in British Columbia. The outfitter had flown to town for the day. His girl friend had gone outside to split some wood, and managed to run the blade of an axe between her thumb and first finger, almost removing her thumb. I sewed it back as best as I possibly could. I had no idea on the proper procedure of sewing, so used the half baseball stitch, such as taxidermists use to sew mounts. Back in Montana, my doctor taught me the proper stitches. He said that packaged pre-threaded needles can be bought. If such an emergency ever arises again, I hope to be better prepared than I was on that occasion.

Footgear

Along with the hunter's rifle, his shoes and socks are his most important equipment. Let one's feet become blistered and sore and your hunt comes to an abrupt end.

I too have suffered from blistered heels. but learned early in my hunting career to take some protective measures. The hunter traveling long distances needs to wear two pairs of socks to protect his feet. Next to my skin I wear cotton and over these I place medium to heavy wool socks. The theory is that by wearing two pairs your feet do not slip and slide inside your shoes. No matter how weary and sore the rest of my body is, I seldom have any problem with my feet. On occasion, I have started out in the morning thinking I was only going for a short hike and ended up making a hard climb. With only a single pair of socks on my feet, invariably my heels will trouble me before the end of the day. WEAR TWO PAIRS OF SOCKS.

When I first started hunting the alpine, in the early 60's, good shoes were hard to locate. Vibram soles were just coming on the market, and most boots did not have them. Today, all manner of shoes have the vibram, or lug type sole. They are nice, but they do not provide traction on steep, wet, grassy hillsides. Hobnails or caulks provide a much better grip over a wider range of conditions, than the lug sole. Nails and caulks are a bit noisy on rocks, but not so bad as you might think.

Another sole that is not commonly found, but has excellent traction is the Air-Bob, which is manufactured in western Montana. It sports a series of flexible half spheres. The sole is not widely distributed and is difficult to install, but those that have had them installed never go back to the lug sole again,

For cold weather, the Canadian type packs with felt liners are excellent and will keep your feet warm, as long as the liners are dried each night.

If one is to attempt climbing icy slopes, or steep wet grassy hillsides, a pair of crampons can come in handy. I have a pair that has been fitted to my boots. The long steel points provide so much traction they can get you into trouble. They can take you upwards to where you can't return.

Another word of advice — avoid buying shoes that are too low. The six-inch-high boots are lighter to wear, but they allow weeds, dead grass and small rocks to enter, any of which can give rise to foot problems. I have found 10-inch top boots ideal. My pant legs cover the tops, preventing the entrance of foreign material.

As the hunter may constantly encounter snow and numerous creeks that need to be crossed, it is imperative that shoes be waterproofed. I have tried all manner of shoe preservatives and have found two that do a superb job for me — Sno Seal and Dri. There are others but this is what I use. To get long lasting protection, I pre-warm my shoes in an oven set on

The author has Air-Bob soles on his favorite hunting boots. They give excellent traction on rocks as well as ice.

low heat. At the same time I melt the Sno Seal or Dri on the stove; then apply it with an old toothbrush. Heat allows the preservative to penetrate the pores of the leather. So treated, my boots will remain waterproof for several days through the most adverse hunting conditions.

Meat And Cape Bags

The backpacking hunter is required by law to salvage for human consumption all meat from game he has killed. Why carry bones? Humans don't eat them, so why break your back carrying them, for miles, when they are going to end up in the garbage can? Once boned, meat needs to be protected from dirt, flies and moisture. For many years my wife made game bags from old bed sheets. They do a nice job of keeping meat clean and free of blow flies, and are porus enough to allow air to circulate. On smaller big game animals such as mountain goats, sheep and deer I sort into either two or three bags. I use one or two bags for steaks and roast, and the other for hamburger type meat. When using three bags, the second is for the chuck and any other meat that could be used for lesser steaks or roast. An additional bag is carried for the cape. By storing it in a bag, I can keep hair from contaminating my meat.

If blow flies aren't a problem, one can use game bags made of very porus materials. My son, Stuart, is working in a large grocery store and he brings home onion bags. They work fine as meat bags. It should be noted that some states require that big game be brought out whole.

Raingear

Rain and snow can be the bane of the hunter. The morning might begin without a cloud in the sky, with an inch of precipitation being dumped before the day is over, on the unsuspecting traveler. Rain gear is a must, unless the traveler can be happy being wet and cold. On one Alaskan sheep hunt, it rained a dozen days on a 12-day trip. To save weight, Harry Johnson and I had bought cheap, throw-away, full-length raincoats. After the second day, the sleeves started to rip away, and by the end of the hunt our rain clothes were in tatters. Well, what does one expect or deserve for $2? I learned my lesson. For a cheap price all you can buy is cheap merchandise.

In 1975, I purchased an expensive set of lightweight rain gear from Recreation Equipment Inc. With judicious patching, my rain suit is still nearly as good as new. The fabric is light so it will not keep you totally dry in a prolonged downpour. If heavy rains are expected, nothing will take the place of heavy duty rain gear like Helley Hanson. If it is raining hard enough to necessitate quality rain cloths maybe one shouldn't be out in the first place, but along the coast the hunter may not have much choice.

Gore-Tex is claimed by many to be the ultimate wet weather fabric. Most persons living on the Alaska coast think that Gore-Tex will not do the job. This past fall, I was given a Gore-Tex suit. Around saltwater it was worthless for it leaked and it did not let perspiration out. I will stick to my Helley Hanson rainclothes. Gore-Tex is reputed to be better now, by some people.

Food For The Trail

I was first introduced to freeze dried food in 1962, soon after moving to Alaska. Gene Dursin and I had been assigned to walk some 12 miles to cruise a timber sale along the Knik River. The Safeway Store in Anchorage was introducing a line of the new freeze dried foods. Gene and I decided to give them a try. When we split the food for the three day trip, we couldn't believe that we would be eating at anything beyond a starvation level. Eat we did, and with full bellies. In fact, we had food left over. I have been using freeze dried foods for years and all I can say is that they are light. They keep one going even if they don't taste the best. It is expensive grub, so always try to supplement its use with other lightweight foods. In my opinion, the Mountain House brand has the most durable packaging, which is so important, for if the container opens you have nothing.

Today, we have many other lightweight products available on grocery store shelves that are a lot cheaper than freeze dried products. Ramen makes a nice substitute for potatoes. I have used many well-packaged, flavored rice mixes, as well as stuffings. Chewey Granola and other breakfast bars are tasty, nutritious and well packaged. Stick to the chewey bars as one dentist told me that the hard bars are a prime breaker of teeth. There are a multitude of lightweight casseroles available. I have also tried packaging my own foods in Seal-A-Meal bags.

Container breakage can be a major problem to the hunter. Once the package opens the contents are lost. For the past 10 plus years, I have been carrying many products in plastic bottles. In them I store: syrup, rice, dried potatoes, coffee, salt, sugar, pancake flour and any other loose products I might need. Since using these containers spillage and loss has been reduced to near zero.

To make life easier, I have been pre-packaging my backpacking food in day bags for nearly two decades. In each bag include enough food for two or three persons for one day; plus matches, toilet paper, a soap pad, instant coffee, paper plates and plastic spoons. Each day's contents are placed in a small plastic garbage bag. Anything that can be water damaged is wrapped in foil. Each year, make enough ration bags to last for the season. On a five day hunt all one needs is to pick up five ration bags and you are ready to go.

Camp Stoves

The hunter to the high country will often be camping above any firewood. If one is backpacking, you need the lightest stove possible, and there are a great many available. I have owned mine since the early 60's, and today it works as well as when purchased. In fact, I used it three times this week. It does not have a pump, so heat is needed to generate pressure. The directions said to hold your hands around the tank to generate sufficient pressure to start the stove. This method has never worked too well, so I always let a few drops of gasoline drip along the sides. As a safety measure, leave the regulator value in the burning position before igniting. When lighted it quickly has all the pressure needed. Maybe the practice isn't too safe, but I have never had any problems. This little stove throws off more heat than my kitchen range, but the flame is too concentrated, especially if turned on a high setting. With judicious use, a gallon of gas will last two people for a ten-day trip. Pressure appliance fuel is expensive, so I often use unleaded auto gas, which is not quite as refined. Never burn leaded gas or your stove or lantern will soon be defunct. NEVER USE UNLEADED GAS IN A CATALYTIC HEATER.

When I want to pack in ultra-light, I carry a tiny alcohol stove that weighs but 3 1/2 ounces. I bought several of these several years ago from Recreation Equipment Inc. for $2.50 each. The stove itself is smaller than a flat of tuna. One must build a ring of rocks around the stove for your frypan or pot to sit on. The only complaint I have with these midget alcohol stoves is that they always seem to run out of fuel just before dinner is cooked. A filling last for an average of 20 minutes. Alcohol is more expensive than gasoline. I usually buy my alcohol in gallon cans as a gas line anti-freeze. Last fall at Icy Bay, Tom Matuska devised a stand for my alcohol stove based on an empty coffee can. He quickly provided air vents with a can opener.

For normal camping, I use both gasoline and propane stoves and lanterns. Before the start of each season, I check them for proper operation. Once every few years you may need to replace a generator.

Author's backpacking stove.

The author is sold on Peak 1 backpacking frames by Coleman. They come in a variety of sizes and external bags.

Miscellaneous Camp Gear and Goodies

Most camp cooking kits come complete with metal cups. Throw them away. Drinking hot liquids from a metal cup is the best way I know to burn your lips. Use an insulated plastic cup. Coffee stays warm and you won't burn your mouth.

As rain is the bane of the hunter, carry ammunition in plastic shell cases. The cardboard boxes ammo comes in never seems to last a trip.

If one is traveling in country where a compass is needed, buy the best, a Silva Ranger. It is compact and yet is capable of rough surveying work. Magnetic declination can be preset, so all readings are true. The card is liquid filled, so the needle settles rapidly, allowing quick precise readings. I have been using mine for 18 years, and with it have run property lines over long distances. It is the best.

All hunters should be well armed with maps; the more detailed the better. In the "Far North", U.S.G.S. maps on a scale of one inch equals one mile are the most popular. Contour lines enable a hunter to accurately plan his hunts. One can predetermine the length of valleys, how rough they are and where the lowest passes are. In the West, in addition to U.S.G.S. maps, one can obtain charts from the Bureau of Land Management and the U.S. Forest Service. Most of these maps do not show contour lines, but they do delineate land ownership and drainages. Most of these charts used to be free, but now may cost a dollar or so. If a person is a good map reader he can tell exactly where he is, at all times. In the West, when hunting public domain (B.L.M.) lands it is important to know that you aren't on private land without permission.

If you use the same map year after year, it is a good idea to protect it with iron on backing. This backing can be purchased from surveyor's supply houses.

Today, the backpacking hunter has a wide choice of pack frames from which to choose. Most are good and price mostly depends on the weight to strength ratio. For tying on large loads, I prefer a board that has lashing studs. These can be hard to find.

For the past year, I have been using a Coleman Peak 1 frame and I am 100 percent sold on it. The frame is molded in one piece from a high impact material called RAM-FLX. It has controlled flexibility to move, bend, and flex with the body. The frame has a multitude of slots allowing various positions for the straps, which also serve as lashing points. I have been securing loads, including meat, with bungee cords instead of rope. The cords are quicker and easier to use, as well being more secure. So far my new frame has been used to carry several boned animals from the hills on my aging shoulders. It is the best frame I have used to date.

Nearly all modern frames come equipped with waist belts, and I consider their use a must when toting heavy loads. They take a great deal of strain from one's shoulders.

Molded G.I. surplus frames used to be popular with hunters as they come with lashing hooks, but they are killers with heavy loads, as the center of gravity is so low. I still have one but it sits in the corner.

The finish of many a fine rifle has been ruined by the mechanical action of a slung rifle's barrel rubbing across the aluminum tubing of a pack frame. All backpacking hunters are plagued by this problem. My good friend Russ Moody devised a solution. He merely tapes on a section of hollow foam pipe insulation onto the frame. The barrel is only contacting the non-abrasive action of the foam.

For cooking pots, I often use old coffee cans. I drill holes in the side and attach handles with stove pipe wire. By using one, two and three pound cans the hiking hunter can make a free set of nesting pots. The price is right.

Another item I always carry is a 1/4-inch steel tape. With it I am able to measure horns and take any needed taxidermy measurements.

My good friend Al Kadush of Juneau, Alaska, devised one of the best weight savers I have heard of. He once suggested, on a goat hunt, we take only one rifle to the the hills. If two men are hunting sheep or goats together, only one can usually shoot at a time anyway, so why tote two rifles. Since that first single weapon hunt, Morrie Giaudrone, my hunting companion, and I have frequenty headed for the alpine with but one rifle.

Using a single weapon never caused a problem, and the concept has saved us packing a lot of unneeded weight.

As a cheap insurance policy, when weight and space allows, it is a good idea to have an extra scope at base camp, along with the proper sized screwdriver to make the change. On my three trips to Africa, I have used a 375 H&H with a low power scope. On these journeys overseas, I have carried a replacement peep sight and a screwdriver in my guncase. I didn't need to make the switch, but I was prepared. On the subject of cases, most serious hunters use aluminum cases while traveling. They will outlast the plastic type by a wide margin.

Fair skinned persons, like myself, should be sure a carry a supply of sun blocking cream.

A piece of plastic (visqueen) is a nice goodie to have along. It can be used as a rain fly over your tent, as a roof on a simple pole leanto, as a waterproof cover over extra gear or as a fly over your meat.

When hunting in the rain or snow, I have found that one can stick Scotch tape to the end of the barrel to keep out any moisture. When you shoot, the tape blows off with no adverse effect on accuracy. I have checked this as I didn't believe it either.

When guiding for Jim Keeline at Icy Bay, Alaska, one of the clients got some dirt down his barrel while hunting goats. After firing a single shot at a billy he was unable to extract his spent case, making his 270 useless.

Author's son, Brian, with a load of sheep meat secured to a Peak 1 frame with bungee cords.

Bighorn ewe cape and a small amount of meat in an onion bag secured to a packframe with a diamond hitch.

Fortunately, the goat was dead, but a small piece of tape would have avoided all his troubles.

Another nice gadget to own is a shooting rest. When I first moved to Montana, I spent a lot of time antelope hunting. The pronghorn, being a dweller of the plains, offers long range shooting. It didn't take long to figure that I should use every aid available to help in making hits. Initially, Russ Moody and I began packing rolled up sleeping bags for rests: a most unhandy proposition at best. I had my wife construct a pillow filled with styrafoam peanuts and covered with a durable fabric. At first, I only carried my homemade rest for antelope hunting, but I soon found that my long range shooting ability improved to such a degree that I now carry it at all times when hunting near a road. The pillow is lightweight, compact and holds its shape in a variety of positions. With it, some of my friends and clients have pulled off some most difficult long range shots. Using a rest I have killed the last seven pronghorns fired at. Several were over 400 yards away.

My son, Brian, uses a day pack filled with styrafoam peanuts for a rest. He is 15 and has killed seven big game animals over the past two seasons.

One final bit of advice: don't camp too close to where you are hunting. I have known more than one mountain hunter who stayed so close to the hunting area that he drove his hoped for trophy over the hill.

Careful handling of the kill in the field enables the hunter to bring his trophy out of the woods in good condition for future mounting, as the author is doing here with a nice bighorn ram.

Chapter Three

SOME THOUGHTS ON FIELD CARE FOR THE BACKPACKING HUNTER

During the past couple of decades there has been a great increase of interest in big game trophy hunting, putting increasing demands on the ever shrinking prime habitats of the game fields of the world. A record book head is considered a premiere accomplishment for the sportsman. Typically, he is willing to spend more money and expend greater effort to reach his end. An ever-larger number of hunters have taken to the hills with a packframe on their back, and an attitude that they will go to where the big ones live.

If one is to hunt long distances from roads, he needs to learn how to reduce a big game animal to minimum size and weight so it can be easily toted on his back to civilization. Having lived in Alaska for better than a decade and a half, plus having roamed the wild country of Montana and Idaho for another 10 years, I have learned most of the tricks of bringing out game the easy way.

After killing several moose for the family larder, it seemed that I was always disgruntled at finding my throwaway boxes contained as much weight as did the boxes of meat for the freezer. Up to that point, I had been subjecting my young body to the punishing task of bringing out a moose, bones and all, in six or seven loads. I finally vowed to quit toting all that excess weight home, only to be later thrown away.

If a person knows he is going to be boning meat, he should carry the proper knife, which has a long thin blade. It allows the butcher to easily cut meat with a minimum of waste.

When I wish to bone an animal, one side of the carcass is first skinned. Next I remove the front shoulder, which can either be packed bone in or

Removing the backstrap.

bone out. Now I direct my knife through the hip joint, keeping my blade as close to the hip bone as possible, so that what is considered the rump roast remains with the ham. Keep the bone in the ham until home; otherwise, this piece of meat is too hard to handle.

As you are cutting, sort the meat into three bags. Into two of the bags, place the shoulders, hams, backstraps and tenderloins. The third is used for the rest of the boned meat, which is of hamburger quality. For bags, I use either regular game bags, onion bags or bags sewed from pieces of old bed sheets.

The remaining meat on the first side of the carcass is now removed bone free. The backstrap is a strip of meat that runs from the hip to the area between the ninth and tenth ribs. This strip is suitable for steaks, or roast, and includes the sirloin and rib steaks. Forward of this point, the strip should be considered suitable for hamburger or sausage only, as is the neck. On smaller big game animals, such as deer, there is little or no usable meat on the ribs. Ribs have enough fat on them that, if frozen, will turn rancid, making them inedible.

The gamy taste one hears about is 90 percent fat that has turned rancid. Game fat should be always be trimmed away before the meat is frozen.

Now that one side has been completed, the carcass may be rolled and the process repeated. Note, I have never mentioned gutting the animal. I haven't either. The only reason to ever gut an animal is to recover the tenderloins — the choicest cut of all.

If an animal is gut shot, why open him up at all. One can bone the carcass and never get any of that rank meat contaminating material on the

The old GI board is a favorite with hunters as it has lashing studs. It doesn't have a waist belt, and the load sits too low which makes its use somewhat difficult.

outside of the body at all. I have saved many an animal in this fashion.

On large animals like moose or elk, I may save part of the rib cage for fresh barbequed ribs.

A moose so cut can be reduced to about five pack loads, and if carefully trimmed will weigh less than 400 pounds. A bull elk can be cut down to about 275 pounds, according to meat cutter Gordon Michens. Last year, I weighed a moderate-sized muley buck, so prepared, at 117 pounds. We have weighed several antelope bucks so reduced at 60 pounds, plus or minus very little. Michens killed a large trophy muley last fall that yielded 105 pounds of boneless meat, with an estimated live weight of 280.

By boning as described, I believe the weight is reduced by 55 percent from the live weight. If it is warm, bags help keep away any flies from meat. Another trick to keep blow flies away is to sprinkle pepper on the meat anywhere that it is damp, like in any folds. If these insects aren't kept away, they lay eggs which will hatch into maggots.

The backpacking hunter should attempt to purchase a frame with lashing studs for tying on loads. Most frames do not have studs, but a few do. Be sure the frame has a waist belt, which helps take much of the weight from your shoulders. Meat, capes, antlers and horns can be tied to a frame, or secured with stretch cords. I prefer cords to rope as they are faster and seem to hold a load better. If rope is used and it starts to loosen, all seems to be lost and soon you will be retying the load.

If you know how to secure the load with a diamond hitch, you will seldom have to retie it. This hitch is most useful for tying a bear hide on a frame, as this is a most difficult item to keep in place. First one foot wants to come loose, then another and finally the hide is on the ground. It is best to put a bear hide in a bag before securing to a frame. For the past two years, I have packed all bear hides secured with bungee cords. The system works well.

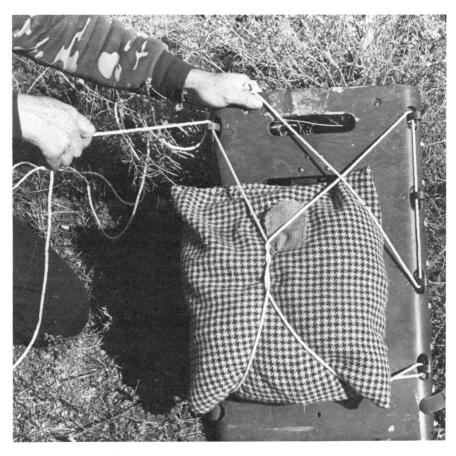

The load has been placed on the packboard. A rope has been run around the bottom studs. At the load's center, twist ends twice around each other. Run the rope ends around the top studs.

Pull the string down to and around the middle studs. The ends now should be brought between the two twists at the center. As you pull, the diamond is formed.

Run the end of the rope back to the center studs, up and over the load, and tie off with a square knot.

Author with western Montana bighorn ram shot by Russell Moody of Hamilton, Montana.

Chapter Four

SOME THOUGHTS ON PHOTOGRAPHY

During the summer of 1955, I worked as a forestry aid for the U.S. Forest Service in the northeast corner of Washington. The ranger district employed an old cowboy-type packer by the name of Urn Curtley. He would entertain us evenings with stories of hunting grizzlies, elk, sheep, mountain goats and other glamorous animals of the Mission Mountains of western Montana. All us young fellows knew Urn must be stretching the truth a whole lot. After all, a man with as many achievements as Urn Curtley claimed would without a doubt be totally famous.

Finally, one evening the old cowboy asked if we would like to see his collection of hunting slides. "Of course we would." Three nights later, after seeing his entire presentation, we were ready to believe anything he told us. We were convinced that Urn must be the world's greatest hunter. I made my vow to always record, on film, the many adventures I hoped that I would someday experience. No one would be able to doubt my tales of adventure when I grew old. In living up to my vow, I have tripped a shutter thousands of times.

During my five-year stint with the Bureau of Land Management (B.L.M), in Alaska, I was able to solve many of the mysteries of photography, and darkroom technique, under the able assistance of Henrietta McCrady (Sam). She ran B.L.M.'s darkroom. At the time, the agency was in need of photographic material for the volumes of reports that were being prepared for Washington, D.C. Fortunately, much of this task fell upon my shoulders.

In one single five-day period, I exposed 107 rolls and packs of film including 35mm, 120 and 4x5. Most of my efforts were with black and white film. Sam taught me the tricks of the trade in the darkroom, so I could get the most from each negative.

After leaving the B.L.M., my camera stayed home more and more. For several years I hardly exposed any film at all. The novelty of the Alaska bush had worn away. By 1970, I had thousands of B&W 8x10's stored in notebooks. I also owned an estimated 5,000 35mm slides stored in photobook pages, by subject. All my negatives were catalogued and stored in envelopes. During the winter of 1972, our home burned to the ground and I lost 99 percent of my slides, photos, and negatives.

Once the shock of the fire was past, I resolved to rebuild my collection of photographic material to bigger and better heights. Since that day, fourteen years ago, I have never lost sight of my objective. Now that a considerable portion of my efforts are directed at writing hunting books, maintaining a top-notch collection of photographs has become even more important. My photos, slides, negatives, movies and VCR tapes are organized and I can find my most obscure exposure in a short time. Over the 30 plus years I have been enjoying photography, I have made many mistakes. At times I learned my lessons slowly. Hopefully I can help you avoid many of my errors and pitfalls.

CAMERAS

With the fine films and equipment available in these times, there is little need for most of us to use a format other than 35mm. Few photographers ever demand prints larger than 8x10 and the 35mm will certainly fill the bill. This size negative can be enlarged to 16x20 and still retain good quality. Only the most advanced photographer has need of the 2 1/4 or larger format. And I doubt that a photographer in this category would be reading these words. In an effort at compactness, many outdoorsmen have turned to the 110 or newer disk cameras. They will supply snapshots, but that is about all. The negatives are too small for anything else. After my house fire, I used a pocket 110 for awhile, when I made backpack hunts. I soon found that I could not obtain quality results.

My friends suggested switching to a compact 35mm like the Rollei 35, which is about the size of a pack of cigarettes. I did and have never been sorry. Today, most manufacturers offer compact rangefinder type 35mm cameras. They are capable of quality work. My Rollei is no longer sold on the new camera market. It measures a tiny 3 5/8 by 2 1/4 by 1 1/4 inches. There should be no excuse to leave it at home. On its carrying strap, I have taped two empty 35mm film canisters. They serve as permanently attached storage containers that will protect film from both dirt and moisture.

At one time I packed a twin lens 2 1/4 inch format Yashica. With it I was able to make large enlargements. My negatives have been blown up to a maximum of 8 feet by 6 feet. Few photographers will ever have this need, so why bother with film sizes over 35mm?

The author's Rollei 35S, despite being a full frame, fully adjustable 35mm, is only slightly larger than a pack of cigarettes.

Rangefinder cameras have the problem that lenses may not be interchanged and closeup photography is difficult or impossible. For closeups and telephoto work a single lens reflex (SLR) is needed, which are much larger than rangefinder cameras. If you are very far back in the hills it is awful easy to leave a SLR behind. Realizing this, in 1978 I purchased the world's first 110 SLR, a Minolta complete with a macro zoom lens. It proved capable of supplying me with all the big game and fish taxidermy closeup study photos I needed, but they are of marginal quality. What can one expect from the tiny 110 negative? Today, I seldom use this 110 SLR. It certainly won't produce many photographs of a quality suitable for book publication.

I still own a Yashica twin lens reflex that uses 127 film, which yields a much larger negative than a 35mm. This camera has not been used for over two years, which should tell you something. I doubt if it will be used during the next two years either, even though I have a good supply of 127 film in the freezer.

Like most modern field photographers, I rely on the 35mm SLR. I use three Minoltas with an array of lenses and accessories. Today, nearly all SLR's manufactured are designed for automatic exposure control. This feature is built around complex circuitry, which is liable to failure when used in the adverse environments roamed by many hunters. The wet coastal habitats where I spend much of my time are absolutely destructive

The Minolta 110 SLR is the smallest single lens reflex found.

to complicated electronics. This past spring (1985), outfitter Jim Keeline obtained a new video outfit. After a few days the camera shorted out, even though it was never taken out directly in the rain. When in the field under adverse conditions, I use a totally manual camera. My Minolta XG7 with an electronic shutter quit, without warning, last week while photographing Herb Klein's Grand Slam at Dallas, Texas. My camera repairman said dirt had foiled the circuits, so I traded my body for a reconditioned XG7 at a cost of $75.

My camera maintenance shop in Missoula, Montana, tells me that if the circuitry goes bad in a programmable camera it is cheaper to buy a new piece of equipment than to repair it.

My personal battery contains three Minolta SLRs: an XG7, an SRT 101 and a SRT 102. The latter two can be operated with no batteries whatever. The XG7 is capable of totally automatic operation, and I like it because with an auto winder I can rapidly expose film, while taking wildlife shots, from either the ground or while flying. Last year my son, Stuart, shot 36 exposures in two passes by a herd of elk in my Super Cruiser airplane. Ed Shoemaker exposed 28 slides of me making a single aircraft takeoff.

I prize my pair of SRT's. Manual SLR's have about gone the way of the Mexican grizzly. The only two currently being manufactured are the Nikon and the Pentax. My 19-year-old son, Stuart, carries a manual Nikon when he roams the hills of western Montana. The boys at my camera shop convinced him of the merits of having 100 percent manual capability. As the demand for adjustable cameras has declined to such a degree, I had mine overhauled in case parts might become unavailable in the future.

I have no real reason for using Minoltas other than I acquired the first in a trade. Before that I carried Exactas, which originally were ahead of most cameras in design. Once they were a fine piece of equipment. For better than a decade, they have been made in communist Germany and are JUNK. My last body lasted less than a year, when the damp air of Kodiak completed its job of creating a piece of nothing.

I believe all the major manufacturers provide a good product, and whatever you finally choose it is only a matter of personal choice. With modern sophistication, the variation in features is slight. In reading camera magazines, you will find there is no consistency in what the pros choose. I have noted that many outdoor photographers buy Nikon. I have been told that they produce an extremely durable camera.

LENSES

The big advantage of the SLR is the ability to change lenses. The photographer of dead trophies, or trophy rooms needs a wide angle. The landscaper wants a mid-range telephoto. The wildlife photographer needs a full telephoto. The copier of past photos or plant photographer should buy a macro lens, or slide copier. The SLR with a selection of optics allows one to achieve all. My personal battery includes: 28, 50, 55, 135, 39-80 and 80-200 plus 1.8X extender, a set of closeup lenses and a slide copier. In the future I hope to add a 400 or 500mm lens. A 50 or 55mm lens is considered normal and with one most people do the bulk of their picture taking.

The 28mm and 35mm optics are wide angle lenses. With them, you can easily photograph home interiors or make dead trophies appear larger than real life. They have a great depth of field and at a mid-range f stop everything from 10 feet to infinity should be in focus. This is the lens to use if you want to make your bear trophy look huge, or you need to take pictures of trophy rooms. As a disadvantage, this lens will distort objects. Closeups of airplanes appear to have wings much too long. Many advanced photographers use the 28mm as their standard lens due to its ability to retain everything in focus.

I have found the 80mm lens to be most useful. It makes mountains appear most like what we think they should look. As it is a telephoto, of sorts, depth of field is shallow, tending to blot out unwanted backgrounds in portrait photography.

My 135 is a quality Minolta lens that opens to f3.5. My 80-200 was purchased at K-Mart and will only open to f5.6. In poor light, it is a marginal lens.

Many years ago when working for the B.L.M., we examined many negatives under a compound microscope. As to resolution, high cost optics didn't always produce the sharpest image. In fact, many inexpensive lenses did as well as those costing many times more. We found that the twin lens Yashica produced images nearly as, or as sharp as, the most expensive optics on the market.

My 1.8 extender will increase the focal length of any lens by 1.8 times, but it also decreases the light gathering properties by 1.8 times. An 5.6 lens becomes nearly an f11.

Mirror telephotos have the advantage that they are more compact than standard optics. On the negative side, they are non-adjustable as to f stops. Most are fixed at f8, which limits their use to sunny days or high speed films.

Macro lenses are exceedingly useful to the outdoor photographer. They allow closeup photos of plants, tracks and reproduction of other photographs. For the latter use, I have found that I will get acceptable copies about half the time. As an alternate, a copy stand is ideal but often the hunter-photographer may have an opportunity to copy a most unusual older picture. I would rather have a 50 percent chance of success than no opportunity at all. Part of the secret is having the photo copied lying absolutely flat. With my closeup lenses, I am constantly copying museum exhibits, old photographs, maps, alpine plants, tracks, dung, spent bullets, etc.

Another copier is the slide duplicator. Some are designed to give 1:1 duplicates while others will crop. They don't do a bad job at all and I have copied many a slide using black and white or color negative film. I know of two outdoor writers whose black and white book illustrations were all originally slides. They are good photographs.

As a rule, zoom lenses do not have the light gathering ability of fixed focal length optics, and most will only open to f5.6. For low light work, it is desirable to be able to open to f2.0 or more.

FILM

Most of my past photography errors have been in the choice of film. Twenty-five years ago, I used either Kodachrome 25 or Plus-X black and white (ASA 125). Today I am using Kodachrome 64, Kodacolor 100 along with TRI-X (ASA 400) to a much lesser degree. Not much change for a quarter century of serious shutter snapping. The trails I have followed in the mid-years led to many dead ends. In the interest of saving a bit of money I have tried some odd films, with offbeat developing. Some of your bargain brands of color print film may save a few pennies but the negatives themselves are thin, and the colors are not true.

Soon after my home burned, I tried several rolls of the then new surplus movie film which offers the supposedly tremendous feature of both slides and negatives. As luck would have it, I picked a processor that went bankrupt and it took over a year to get some of my film back. The quality of their work was terrible, and it was obvious that they commonly used dirty chemicals. I didn't try 5247 again until four years ago. This time I really stocked up; after all, my good friend Allen D'Aigneau liked it. Fifty rolls later, I quit for the second time. Many slides returned with a dirty haze over them. Others were spotted. The negatives cannot be made into prints by the normal lab, or they won't. Labs that would do the work often took 60 days. What is wrong with having prints made directly from slides? Print film in a slide copier is also a way for the advanced photographer to get prints. At one time prints from slides were not of the quality of prints from negatives, but now-a-days I think there is little difference. Allen and I added up the tally. Between us, we had prints made from a total of six 5247 negatives; hardly a reason to put a combination of slides and negatives on the plus side of the ledger. I have learned that magazine editors generally automatically reject any material submitted with non-standard films.

Today, so few people use B&W film most processing labs don't like to handle it. For the past few years, I have found that one must either develop it himself or send it to a custom lab, which is fairly expensive. For book and magazine illustrations, I was always told that B&W is nearly a must. Don't believe it; a quality color print will make a good B&W illustration. Very little is lost in the transition. Recently, I was looking at a new hunting book with the publisher, and all the B&W illustrations originated as color slides. Some of the pictures were of marginal quality but so were the transparencies.

I still use some B&W film and will continue doing so, as one can produce some dramatic effects in the darkroom.

Some people expose so much film that cost is a consideration. I order rolls by the dozen from the discount houses listed in the various photo magazines. I am done experimenting with my slides. Buy Kodak film with Kodak processing, or Fuji with Fuji processing.

Don't get me wrong. There are non-Kodak films that are of high quality. I have used many myself with perfect results, especially Fuji.

TRIPODS

I have always felt that most photographers do not get the full potential from their equipment. Is it logical to own a top quality lens and then hand hold the camera? I don't think so! The old rule is do not try and hand hold at slower shutter speeds than the reciprocal of the focal length of the lens, i.e. don't hand hold a 50mm lens with any shutter speed less than 1/50 of a second, or a 250mm lens at less than 1/250 of a second. To get absolutely the best pictures a tripod is desirable. With a tripod, it becomes possible to use a self-timer and get into the picture yourself. A full-sized tripod is pretty much of a luxury for the sportsman. They are generally too large and bulky for most situations. I own a mini-pod that weighs but ounces. It doubles as a window pod for any camera or spotting scope, and also allows the luxury of photographing myself when I am in the field alone, which is often. Mine came from LaBelles for $9.95, but other companies offer them too. For serious wildlife photography, consider the use of a full-size tripod a must, but the mini-pod will work to a lesser degree when the larger instrument can't be carried. Remember, the mini-pods do not have extendable legs.

TECHNIQUES

I would like to pass on a few tricks learned over the years. The sportsman traveling to Alaska and northern Canada will generally be transported through some magnificent country via bush plane. Here is your chance to obtain some spectacular mountain and glacier photos. Satisfactory results can be obtained shooting directly through plexiglass windows. Clean windows, of course, are best but dirt and scratches make less difference than you would think. Fast shutter speeds are a must. I try and use 1/1000 of a second, but under poor light conditions I often expose film at 1/500 of a second. Try a slower shutter speed and you will probably end up with a bunch of blurry pictures. All aerial movies should be taken at slow motion speeds. I have a lot of movie filming experience and, believe me, most movies taken at normal speeds from an airplane will leave the viewer airsick.

Most people try to avoid letting any part of the wing get into a picture. Actually a properly positioned wing or strut can act as a frame and can add beauty and interest to the photograph. I often purposely add a portion of the wing in composing. After all, the photo was taken from an airplane.

Photographing dead game is an art in itself and a skill few hunters and guides understand. I used to think that I knew what was going on until my first safari to Africa. Some white hunters really know how to pose hunters with game. As they are responsible for such large quantities of trophies being collected, they have lots of opportunities for practice.

Expose for the subject. Often the trophy will be much darker in color than the background. A general area light meter will give the proper overall light setting, but it may be off for you, and or, the trophy. If in doubt, take several shots at different settings (bracketing). Sometimes a picture taken at the extreme end of bracketing will turn out best. Snow can be particularly troublesome.

Try and wipe away as much blood as possible, on the side that will be showing. A bloody trophy looks in poor taste even to another hunter, let alone a nonhunter.

A strobe light can often save the day if your trophy is taken late in the day, when the light is failing. Use a strobe for fill in light; to minimize shadows. Many a photograph has been nearly ruined because of strong shadows. Be aware of shadows and try to position the photographer, and the animal, to minimize or eliminate them. Commonly the photographer will goof by casting his own shadow into the picture. BEWARE! Watch the shadows!

After many years, I finally learned to position horn/antler tips against the sky when possible. If the hunter's body is behind the horn or antler, the impressiveness of the trophy is reduced. The tips need to stand out. The same holds true if the tips are lost in a clutter of brush or vegetation. Attempt to keep your hands away from the horns or antlers. Support the trophy under the chin, or in some other manner other than partially blocking the full magnificence of the trophy itself.

Most hunters take their dead game photos from too great a distance. Generally, trophies look best shot from close in. Many of the most dramatic photos will not even include the entire animal. If the subject doesn't stretch across at least 80 percent of the picture as a rule you are too far away. MOVE IN.

In order to compose many of the more dramatic hunting pictures, shooting at a low angle is necessary, which tends to bring obstructing vegetation into view. Take the time to pull out, or cut away, unwanted matter. You may have just collected a trophy of a lifetime, so five extra minutes in getting ready for that special photo should not be considered too time consuming.

Many of the finest trophy pictures are taken with a 28mm wide angle lens. Perspective is lengthened, combined with increased depth of field. This is how those dramatic photos are taken of giant bears that look to be nearly as large as elephants. The hunter kneels just behind the trophy, posed head on. The lengthening effect of the wide angle lens makes the

The author and his son, Stuart, with Morrie Giaudrone's white rhino. Notice how the photographer cast a strong shadow across the rhino.

Author caping a Dall ram.

Author's young son, Brian, approaching his fallen bighorn ewe. Photos such as this are a welcome change from the usual dead trophy photos.

hunter appear small in relation to the bear while keeping both the bear and the hunter in focus. This is a great system anytime you want to maximize the apparent mass of an animal, or his headgear.

A couple of years ago I enjoyed an alligator hunting trip to Louisiana with Gene Joanen and Jerry Fabacher. As they were commercially pursuing gators, I had many chances to photograph their catches. I wasted a lot of film before I determined the most spectacular way to photograph a gator. The hunter should kneel behind the animal laid lengthways with a good bend to the tail. A mid-range wide angle (approximately 35mm) will help keep everything of interest in focus. I think my best shots were when the alligator's tail was to the front of the photo.

Some interesting kill photos can be taken as a deviation from the standard of a hunter with a dead animal. Try shots of the fallen trophy in the foreground with the hunter approaching his prize in the background. Use your imagination. I do. One of my best photos is of me caping a Dall ram.

This has by no means been a complete course on photography for the hunter, but you should have gained some food for thought.

Chapter Five

SOME THOUGHTS ON GLASSING

I had lived in Alaska but a short time and already embraced ideas of being a great, if not at the least a better than most, big game hunter. My success had been a bit better than average when a coworker, named Howard, decided to take me under his wing. My mentor was at least 15 years older than me and had a reputation as a hunter with wide experience. It was moose season and we decided to hunt some 70 miles east of Anchorage on some semi-open birch and spruce benches. This was great black bear and moose habitat and I could generally find a moose or two on a day's hunt. I was not prepared for the large number of animals my teacher was able to show me that day — game that I would never have seen if he had not pointed them out to me. On this day I vowed to work at being a hunter; a hunter that is able to make his own luck.

What did I learn that day from Howard? I found the secret of being a successful glasser is to be constantly using your binoculars, looking into every spot where your quarry might be. The unitiated tends to stop at some overlook and spend five minutes gazing at the scenery through his binoculars rather than studying prime habitat. You need to be able to recognize prime habitat. Binoculars should be but an extension of your eyes.

Binoculars are referred to as 6x30, 7x35, 10x50, etc. The first number indicates the magnification and the second the diameter of the objective lens, in millimeters. The ratio of the two squared measures the relative brightness. A pair of 6x30's, 7x35's or 10x50's would all be 25, but 7x50's would be rated at 50. In good light there isn't any major difference in the brightness between various optics, but during first and last light, the

Author's Leupold 9x35 binoculars.

hunter's prime times, there is a world of difference. There is but one problem, in order to have brightness binoculars must be massive and heavy. When one is glassing from a road, weight means little, but when the sportsman is hiking to the back country weight becomes important.

I own several pairs of glasses. The pair I normally use are Leupold 9x35's. They are medium weight binoculars that allow me to see much better in poor light than my naked eye is able to resolve. The reason I like these glasses so well is that each eyepiece is individually focused with click stop adjustments. They seldom get out of kilter. I bought mine at a discount house for $135 and I believe you can never go wrong with a Leupold product. Cheap glasses are always in need of refocusing, which after a few hundred times during the day can get quite exasperating.

My good friend Larry Hilton likes to spend long periods from a set location. He uses a large pair of 10x70 Fuji's, allowing him to almost see game in the dark. One would never want to carry these optics far, but they are a wonderful glass for what he uses them for.

Today, there are a multitude of lightweight binoculars on the market, which are fine for the hunter, as long as he does not need to glass under poor light conditions. For example, the 8x20 Redfield only weighs 6.8 ounces. By comparison Redfield 10x50's tip the scale at 29 ounces.

As a bit of advice, I don't think much of zoom binoculars. They are heavy and I have yet to see a pair that were clear on the upper power settings. I get used to judging animals, like bears, at a given power and become completely confused using zoom glasses.

Without a doubt, the Leitz is the Cadillac of all glasses, with a price of over $500 for the 8x40, even at a discount house. I have never owned a pair but a friend lent me pair for my 1978 safari. Once focused, they stayed set. They produced zero eye fatigue, even after prolonged glassing sessions. Zeiss is also top of the line.

The novice with binoculars generally will throw them to his eyes and quickly announce there isn't an animal on the hill. The expert glasser looks with a system, spending much time tearing apart prime habitats. One must be able to pick out parts; maybe an ear, or a single antler, or maybe a rump. The off-white of a mule deer or bighorn sheep rump often stands out long before any other part is seen. Coues' deer like to lay at the shady base of a cactus. Mountain goats are nearly always a

Author intently glassing a Montana hillside for mountain goats. Most of his time is being spent watching the lushest grass where a billy would have the easiest time filling his belly.

yellowish or dirty white, depending upon their environment. Pure white spots seldom prove to be mountain goats. The only way a person becomes an expert glasser is to glass.

Many a hunter has told me that he doesn't need binoculars as he can use his 3x9 rifle scope. Hogwash! No man can methodically study the countryside with a rifle scope, as he can with binoculars. I have seen a 100 deer on a hillside where a short time before other hunters had driven by and seen nothing.

Most effective hunters glass with a method. Some work from top to bottom, or from far away to close in. All truly good hunters spend the bulk of their time looking at prime habitat. Two weeks ago while fishing in the Montana backcountry, along the Idaho border, Walt Easley and I saw two bands of mountain goats. One was conspicuously bedded on a patch of snow, while the other was lying on broken rock the identical color as their pelage. We knew where they were resting, but were unable to see them without our binoculars, even though we were only about 600 yards away.

Even with glasses, the hunter needs to know what he is looking for. Mule deer and bighorn sheep are usually first seen from the rear because of their light-colored rumps. Mountain goats are lightish, but not usually white, as they take on the color of the surrounding dirt. When bedding on shale they can become quite darkish.

With the exception of pronghorns, caribou, Dall sheep and goats in some areas, North American big game animals are seldom seen far from cover. Most generally, big game is spotted near the edges and that is where the hunter should spend the bulk of his time looking. There is many a bush wise outdoorsman who can discern more with his naked eye than others can with glasses.

In the spring, I spend many hours studying slides looking for black bear. It seems that anytime I need binoculars to determine if it is a bear, it isn't. When a blackie appears, I always instantly say "There's a bear". A black bear seems to have a certain gleam, about its fur, that a log, stump or rock lacks.

Many times the hunter is only able to see a small portion of an animal, and if it is bedded it can be most difficult to ascertain what it is. If that suspicous-looking object doesn't move after a reasonable period, continue glassing and come back to that would-be animal. In a few minutes time one may have several potential animals to check. Sometimes what, after detailed studying, is determined to be a bush or rock has suddenly walked away. Once I even stalked a barrel thinking it was a grizzly. No kidding, I even had it squared as a seven and a half footer. I have a medium sized caribou rack displayed in my workshop that I first determined to be a willow bush. The bush ran until I was able to recover from my astonishment and fire a shot from my 375 H&H.

Lens protectors will keep rain and snow from obstructing one's binoculars.

Fully or even more important to the trophy hunter as his binoculars is a spotting scope. This is especially true of the sportsman on the open plains in parts of the West, or high country, where a mile can take hours to reach. A spotting scope can save hours of slow, hard climbing for the mountain hunter who is after a mighty ram, a billy, or maybe a giant

Author using a spotting scope to study bighorn rams in the high country of western Montana.

buck. Binoculars just won't do the job on many occasions. A scope is a necessity for accurate trophy judging.

Two days ago I was bighorn sheep hunting with my friend, Russ Moody, in the mountains of western Montana. We had foolishly left the scope in camp as the weather was sour with frequent snowstorms. We little expected to find any rams. With visibility reduced to less than a half mile, we discovered nine rams in a sheltered pocket. After an hour of studying in poor light with 9X binoculars. we decided that one ram was close to book size. On the ground it was, but the horn length was less than estimated and the base was greater. With a scope I could have done a much better job.

Many back packing hunters, in the interest of saving weight, leave the tripod at home. I do too. Years ago I found that the hunter could get by with resting a scope on a rock, padded with a jacket, if it had a 45 degree eyepiece. This feature allows the hunter to look down into his scope. Today, one can buy a mini pod for about $10 so there is little reason to go without some sort of tripod. When near the road I much prefer to mount my spotting scope on a full sized tripod.

Over much of the West the antelope and mule deer hunter is hunting from his vehicle allowing the scope to be mounted on a window mount. The window mount allows accurate trophy judging without ever opening the door. My mount is a Bushnell and cost less than $50. I consider this

A spotting scope with a 45-degree eyepiece high in mountains of the Brooks Range of northern Alaska.

accessory a must for the serious trophy antelope hunter.

Spotting scopes are getting more refined all the time. My 20X Bushnell was purchased in 1972 is 16 3/4 inches long and weighs 48 ounces. My newer 20X Weaver with a 45 degree eye piece is only 12 1/2 long and weighs a much lighter 36 ounces. The new 30X Ultra Light Redfield is an amazing 7 1/2 inches long and a mere 11 1/2 ounces. The 25X Redfield which was recently introduced is eight inches long. What with modern technology I wish I didn't already own two spotting scopes.

Most hunters feel that 20X is all that can normally be used. With higher power the field is too small and except for ideal conditions mirage becomes too serious of a problem. Once in a while 30X is useful, but I have never seen a time when anything over 40X could be classed as anything but a blur. I have never owned a zoom spotting scope because I feel that the higher powers are so seldom used. If weight is not a consideration then by all means purchase the heavier zoom scope.

Because of the scope's restricted field of view they should not be normally used for locating game. The scope is an instrument for judging big game head gear.

Chapter Six

SOME THOUGHTS ON FIELD CARE OF TROPHIES

Traveling over the game fields of the world, I have run across a problem that is common to both sportsmen as well as to guides and outfitters — they don't know enough about the field care of trophies. I have met hunters high in the mountains of Alaska who had just downed a Dall ram, and did not know how to turn the ears or split the lips. Once on a guided trip to Wyoming, with one of the state's best-known outfitters, I was surprised to find that none of his help could cape. How many guides or fishermen know how to take measurements, skin and preserve a fish? The answer is very few. In 1985, I wrote and published a book entitled *The Big Game Hunter's And Fisherman's Complete Guide To The Field Care Of Trophies.* This spiral bound text should aid every sportsman who has aspirations of ever getting a few specimens mounted.

Most big game trophies wind up as full shoulder mounts, and thousands upon thousands of hunters and guides are able to skin the cape to the point where the head is removed from the body. Here is where the going gets tough. Beware! Many amateurs do not retain enough body skin when caping. The initial cut should be rearward of the brisket and preferably behind the front legs. Pull the front legs to the rear to be certain that that the initial cuts are being made far enough back. Sometimes I merely ring the upper leg with my pocket knife, then complete the main cut behind the front legs. Either technique is acceptable.

The main incision is up the back of the neck. Once one has cut to the area behind the antlers or horns, the skinner has to make a T, Y or inverted L cut to the bases. The hide can either be pried away from the base of each horn/antler with a blunt instrument, like a screwdriver, or skinned

Initial skinning cut with the legs ringed.

Using the "Y" cut between a deer's antlers.

away. Be sure to keep the cutting edge of the knife on the underside of the hide. This prevents one from cutting any hair.

Next the skinner cuts through the ear butt with his knife, which can be a small to large opening depending on how close one is working to the skull. The caper now needs to work on the eyes, which presents the most critical part of the entire skinning process. There is no way to make a neat repair of a cut eyelid. BE CAREFUL. Once you reach the eyelid, use the fingers of the free hand to grasp the lid. Using your fingers as a protective guide, you should not cut the lid by mistake. Many big game animals, such as deer, have tear ducts in front of the eye. To keep from damaging this appendage it must be pried from its depression in the skull. This can be either done with the point of your knife, or with a prying instrument, such as a screwdriver.

Skinning the eye of a bighorn ewe.

Skinning the lips.

Once you have completed working around the eyes, continue skinning towards the muzzle. About 1/3 of the distance from the eye to the nose you will come to the inner lips. As you cut through you may mistakenly think that you have created a hole. Care should be taken that the inner lips remain on the hide rather than the skull. The taxidermist will need this skin later, for stuffing into the lip slots of the form.

Upon reaching the nose you will find that there is a section of cartilage between the skull and the tip of the nose. I prefer to leave a bit of this material attached to the hide, to be removed later.

Now that the cape is free of the carcass, including the skull, we still have several steps to complete: split the lips, turn the ears, fine turning the nose, fleshing, salting and drying. Many a hunter can cape except for splitting the lips and turning the ears. Neither is that difficult. Begin splitting at the rearmost section of the inner lips. They are cut beginning at the inside edge. Hold that portion of the lip being worked on between your thumb and index finger. The knife's edge can be easily controlled when it is between your fingers. Only a small thin blade should be used. Proceed all the way around the lips in this fashion. The upper lips always seem easier to work on than the lower ones. DO NOT cut away any lip material as the taxidermist will need it later. This is not a difficult task and I can complete most any big game animal in about five minutes. DO NOT cut all the way through the lips. Stay back about a 1/16 of an inch from the edge.

The nose is ready to be cut free.

Splitting the lips.

The lips are split and turned.

Begin turning the ears by pulling the skin away from the cartilage with finger pressure and short cuts with your knife. At the butt end of the ear, the skin must be separated from the cartilage entirely by knife work. What you are attempting to accomplish is to turn the ear inside out. As one moves towards the tip it is much easier to turn. On smaller big game animals much can be done with the aid of your thumbnail. As a help in turning, place the ear over the end of a screwdriver handle, or kitchen knife handle. The ear can be turned all the way to the tip with your knife, but the process is needlessly slow. Most ears can be turned using more rapid methods. It should be skinned with a knife for at least a quarter of its length before changing methods.

My favorite ear turning tool is a round pointed common kitchen knife. After the lower ear has been split, one is able to manipulate a knife between the cartilage and the skin. To keep from poking the kitchen knife through the skin guide the tip of the blade with your thumb and index finger. If one can work to within 1/8 of an inch from the edge in this manner, you should be able to turn the remaining distance with your thumbnail. Some ears turn easily using a kitchen knife, such as those of antelope, mountain goat and deer. Others like black bear must be skinned with a knife the entire way.

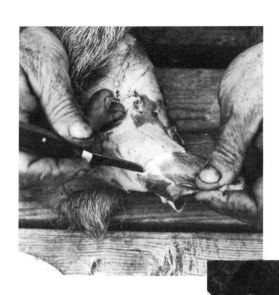

Three views of turning an ear.

Skinning the nose.

The nose needs to be completed. If salt does not reach all parts of the skin there will be spoilage and the epidermis will slip. The nose is split much as the lips.

The cape must be fleshed like any other hide. All meat and fat must be removed. SALT CANNOT PENETRATE FAT. Fleshing may be done with any type of knife you have, but a regular fleshing blade is the fastest. The thin layer of meat in the facial area does not have to be 100 percent removed, but always bear in mind the limits of salt penetration. Some people crosshatch the facial flesh to improve salt penetration. I think a proper fleshing job is best.

Some species have a few special points to remember. Do not flesh around a mountain goat's chin whiskers, or they will likely fall out. Moose have bells that must be split or they will rot away. Caribou bulls during the rut have a dewlap that must be split, or there will be spoilage. Dall sheep have hollow absorbent hair that will easily discolor if blood is allowed to dry. Capes with hollow hair should have all blood washed out before salting and drying.

In Dall sheep country, it is usually cool, so rapid spoilage is not a problem. I have often tied a cord through the eye openings and submerged the skin in a running creek for a few hours. Flowing water keeps hair flexing, which helps flush away any blood. Stained Dall skins must be bleached, which is hard on the hair.

A folded cape.

It is now time for salting. Remember, use fine salt. Flake and stock salt are marginal, but OK if plenty of care is used. I realize either is cheap and that is why so many hunters use it. Table salt is better and the baker's type is best. DON'T USE ROCK SALT. Salt dissolves, pulling moisture from the skin, drawing the hide around the hair roots.

After the cape or hide is laid flat on the ground flesh side up, rub salt into every corner. If it isn't rubbed in by hand, areas may be missed. Small capes like deer and pronghorn need about three pounds of salt at a minimum, but five is better. The muzzle should be folded back onto the neck with the flesh sides of the neck being laid together. The cape is now rolled for storage, out of the sun.

After a day or two, the cape or hide is unrolled and drained of any excess moisture. Check for any unsalted areas. It is now retreated, which takes about half as much salt as the first time. It is now ready for storage. I have kept hides so treated for years. IF YOU ARE NOT GOING TO HAVE IT MOUNTED, DO NOT GET THE SKIN TANNED, for after tanning the mounting life is usually short (about a year). I have seen dry salted hides that were stored 25 years that still tanned beautifully. Some taxidermists differ with my thoughts but most agree.

In conclusion, this chapter is not trying to replace the taxidermist. Unless you really know what you are doing, let your taxidermist cape your trophy, but if there is a chance of the cape spoiling before you can reach help try caping it yourself. If the weather is cool an animal should keep several days without skinning. Better yet, why not practice on a couple of animals that you aren't going to mount.

Montana bighorn sheep.

Chapter Seven

SOME THOUGHTS ON WILD GAME FOR THE LARDER

For me, a part of the thrill of my many years of bush living has been the enjoyment of the many fine foods one finds to eat in the backcountry. Tonight we enjoyed a stew made from my wife's Montana moose of two seasons ago. With double wrapping, the meat was still in perfect condition. Last night we enjoyed a delicious main course of deep fried salmon from fish I caught in Alaska last fall. This afternoon we snacked on smoked brook trout that we caught earlier this week. When I take a break in a few minutes from my computer, I am going to enjoy a bowl of apple sauce from local semi-wild apples. In this chapter, I am going to share with you a few of the recipes and wild foodstuffs that we especially enjoy.

HOT BROTS

This recipe was given to me by Wally Scott, who was the co-owner of First Montana Title Company of Hamilton, Montana. It is a great tidbit for parties, and I have made it several times myself.

2 pounds of Polish game or similar sausage
2 tablespoons cooking oil (optional)
1 cup beer
1/4 cup brown sugar
1/4 cup vinegar
4 teaspoons of cornstarch
1/4 cup prepared mustard
4 teaspoons horseradish

Brown the sausage, draining excess fat. Place in crock pot along with beer, brown sugar and cornstarch. Blend in vinegar, mustard and horseradish. Simmer over low heat all day.

••

LYNN HILDRE'S FISH CAKES

Lynn has spent most of her life in bush camps along the coast of Alaska. She is a true lady of the wilderness. This is one of her favorite taste treats.

2 pounds halibut or other fish
3 eggs
1 medium onion (ground)
1 can pimento (ground)
1 pint milk
4 tablespoons flour
1 teaspoon nutmeg
Enough salt to thicken

Put fish in fine bladed grinder. Beat with electric mixer. Add onion and pimento along with the other ingredients. Add salt last. Brown in butter and place in buttered casserole. Steam over low heat.

••

SMOKING

Most people who live in the bush do a certain amount of smoking meats and fish and I am no exception. I am not going to cover the art in this short chapter, but because so many people ask me, I am going to include a couple of favorite formulas.

MY STANDARD
5 pounds salt
1 pound brown sugar
17 grams pickling spice (a box)
2 tablespoons garlic powder
Use this formula for a dry cure and a brine for both smoked fish and jerky.

JIM KEELINE'S JERKY BRINE
Jim Keeline is a longtime Alaska resident and guide who has plenty of bush savvy. When I worked for him during the fall of 1984, we made several batches of mountain goat and moose jerky using this recipe. **For a 1 quart mix combine 1/2 part soy sauce, 1/4 part A-1 sauce, 1/8 part Heinz 57 sauce, 1/8 part barbecue sauce and 2 tablespoons pepper.** Soak thin slices of meat in this mixture overnight then smoke as you would normally brined meat.

SALMON TIDBIT

During the fall of 1984, Andre and Yvonne Veluire from France hunted with us at Icy Bay, Alaska. They prepared a nice tidbit from coho salmon that we all enjoyed. Slice some salmon or large trout as thin as you can. If it is semi-frozen, so much the better. Soak for several hours in a mixture of lemon juice and cracked coriander. The result is delicious on crackers.

··

ED SHOEMAKER'S HOTCAKES

During the spring of 1985, bush-wise Ed Shoemaker from southern California spent over two weeks with us hunting bear on the Gulf Coast of Alaska. He had many ideas on making life more pleasant, among them two ways to improve Bisquick pancakes. One morning he had us add beer instead of water. All hands thought the pancakes were greatly improved. Another morning Ed added a half can of corn to the mixture sufficient for three persons. The result was most tasty.

··

TERIYAKI

As I have said many times previously, my favorite taste treat is cubes of choice wild sheep, or other big game, soaked in teriyaki sauce. The result is broiled on a stick over an open fire. Any wild or domestic meat can be used, as how often will the hunter have wild sheep available? I generally use the round and cut it into approximately one inch cubes. The sauce can be bought as either a liquid, or a powder. When backpacking, I use the powder otherwise the liquid is just fine. The meat should be soaked for a minimum of a half hour before cooking. We generally heat the remaining sauce for dipping the cooked meat. At home we often cook our meat on skewers under a broiler.

··

PAT'S HAWAIIAN DINNER

This recipe will serve six persons. Saute in margarine 2 pounds wild game round steak cut into bite-sized pieces.
Add one chopped large onion
a chopped green pepper
1 cup chopped celery
16 oz. can of pineapple chunks with juice
2 packages of frozen Hawaiian vegetables
Cook for 15- 20 minutes. Add two packages sweet and sour sauce mixed as directed. Cook until thickened. Serve over rice.

PAT'S HAMBURGERS AND TOMATO SAUCE

Mix 2 pounds hamburger with 1 package dry onion soup and 2 eggs. Form into patties. Fry until almost done. Pour 1 large can tomato soup over the patties and simmer for 10 minutes. Serves 6. This is one of Dunc's favorites.

WILD GAME LONDON BROIL

A real London Broil is made from a beef tenderloin, but as many big game animals are much smaller than an average beef we use backstraps, or a portion of one. Soaking in teriyaki before cooking is optional, and we generally do. Wrap strips of bacon around the meat to help replace the lack of natural fats, and broil to desired degree. We like ours medium rare. When done, slice thin and serve with a side dish of fried mushrooms and onions. People who claim they don't like wild meat generally eat this treat with gusto.

CANNED SMOKED TROUT AND JERKY

I always like to have something extra special for guest in the way of a tasty tidbit. I have found that smoked fish and jerky goes over well. I fillet my trout before smoking to eliminate as many bones as possible, as well as to speed up the smoking process. If I plan on canning the trout or jerky, I smoke the product about half to 2/3 as long as normal. When canning I place 1/2 tablespoon of vegetable oil in each pint jar, along with the meat or fish. I segregate my jerkies and fish by species and mark the jars accordingly. Not a bad gift idea either.

BARBECUED SALMON

A specialty of our oldest daughter, Dotty, is barbecued salmon. It is bound to arouse the taste buds of even those that don't usually enjoy fish. Dotty places the filleted chunks of salmon on the backyard grill and when partly cooked brushes on a sauce that is made of half margarine and half brown sugar. This combination forms a most delicious glaze. Be sure to coat both sides of the fish with vegetable oil before placing on grill. Cover the fish while cooking, as this will help keep the coals from igniting and burning the fish.

The sauce is made by cooking over a low heat a mixture of 1/2 margarine and 1/2 brown sugar, stirring until the mixture is quite thick.

SOME NOTES ON THE CARE OF WILD GAME

GAMEY TASTE

We believe that the objectionable flavor that sometimes wild game is cursed with is due to either improper cooling of the carcass or in the failure to remove the fat. Wild big game fat turns rancid if put in the freezer and imparts a most unpleasant taste. We trim all surface fat away. Ribs, as they contain a great amount of fat, are totally unsuitable for freezing. They are OK when fresh, but that is all.

HAMBURGER

Most people age wild meat, but if it is to be made into burger the process is entirely unnecessary and undersirable. Aging tenderizes meat and so does the making of hamburger. Almost as a matter of habit, with wild game tending to be lean, people add fat from domestic animals to their burger. Beef fat (suet) will turn rancid in time and imparts a bad taste. Pork fat doesn't seem to have quite the undesirable qualities of suet, plus it helps hold the meat together better in pattie form. For the best in game burgers add 30 percent pork trimmings.

TENDERIZING

We all like tender meat that will nearly cut under the weight of a fork. Trophy animals, being by their nature older, will often be tough. The tradtional manner to tenderize meat is to grind it into burger. Another time-honored method is the use of a cube steak machine. I have even put in several small pieces of meat, which will come out as a single cubed steak. Last fall, Gordon Michens, a meat cutter in Hamilton, Montana, introduced me to the needle tenderizer. It is a small machine that contains three rows of 10 needles, and only cost $35. The device will tenderize even the toughest of steaks and roast. As Gordie says, "Why buy expensive cuts when all you need is a needle tenderizer?" Along the same line, I have used a fork to pierce a tough piece of meat multiple times and done almost as good a job.

DEEP FRIED FISH

We have become great fans of deep fat-fried fish and have found that the secret of good flavor is in the batter. Cut the boneless fish into inch cubes. Our favorite species are halibut, ling cod or large trout. Pat has found that fritter batter works best as it tends to soak into the fish itself, providing good adhesion plus adding flavor.

Sift together

1 cup flour

1 teaspoon baking powder

1 teaspoon salt

Beat until fluffy

2 eggs

Add

2 teaspoons of sugar (optional)

1 cup milk

1 teaspoon oil

Chapter Eight

SOME THOUGHTS ON TROPHY ROOMS

The greatest problem most hunters face when building a trophy room is the gathering of design concepts. Few hunters are lucky enough to be able to study several trophy rooms before they start their own. In this chapter I will attempt to provide a few ideas that others have incorporated into their rooms.

At the turn of the century, high-walled Victorian style homes were the norm in our society, but alas this was before the advent of serious big game trophy collecting. Today, eight-foot walls are almost universal, in the interest of lower construction and heating cost. Can a hunter's trophy room be designed around the contemporary eight-foot wall? Yes, if we omit the larger head mounts such as moose, elk, caribou and some of the African species. Nine feet is better than eight, and higher is better yet. Twelve feet is about the maximum you can use. If your room boasts 11 feet or higher walls, you will be able to hang a double row of the smaller trophies like deer, antelope or mountain goat. Adding a little bit of wall height can potentially double the number of heads you can display. The serious trophy collecting hunter needs a display height of at least 11 feet.

How to finish trophy room walls to best display your heads should receive considerable thought. A little preplanning at this time can save later frustrations. Many hunters install walls much too dark. Only white trophies (mountain goat, Dall sheep and polar bear) look good hanging on dark paneling, such as walnut. Most big game animals are either brown, gray or blackish in color calling for a light to neutral background. Natural pine walls can hardly be beat. Driftwood paneling or real barnboards are nearly ideal as a background for most big game species. All but

Rope molding.

A deer antler door handle.

the world's few white animals look fine displayed on a whitish wall of sheetrock, either textured or untextured. I finished one sheetrocked wall with a mixture of plaster and white sand. The mixture was applied in a haphazard manner, moving the trowel every which way. Today, the result remains as an unpainted, inexpensive and attractive background for a multitude of African trophies.

If your room is to be rustic instead of using commercial molding, rope can be used most effectively. I have seen hemp rope used many times in diameters ranging from 3/8 of an inch to a full two inches. I have commonly applied 5/8-inch rope in my construction endeavors. To make rope look more rustic it should be slowly drawn through a flame to burn away any fuzz, and to color the rope a used brown. I have done this over either an open outdoor fire or with a torch. To keep the ends from unraveling you need to secure them in some way. Whipping with thread looks the best, but it is slow. Black plastic tape is a fast way to whip an end.

When rope is hung horizontally it must be nailed closely, or it will soon sag. Three-quarter-inch rope will require securing with a finish nail about every three or four inches.

What could be more appropriate than using handles and supports of antlers and horns. Once cut to shape and size, they need to be drilled to accept nails or screws.

I think most of us have admired hand-hewed beams at one time or another. Few artisans of this era are skillful enough with an axe to effectively hew a beam. Happy days; you can get the full effect without so much as lifting an axe. With a bit of practice, hand-hewed beams and post can be created with a grinder. How nice they look compared to merely staining a rough-cut timber. I urge you to practice on some waste pieces of lumber, so you can discover the various effects that can be achieved with a grinder.

Post and beams are usually stained, commonly a dark brown to simulate walnut. I have found that many stains are too dark to look like real walnut, oak or whatever. I thin my stain with a solvent before applying. It then becomes possible to achieve any degree of darkness desired.

A simulated hewed beam.

When designing my last trophy room, I decided to build a wall with one-inch tongue and groove boards installed diagonally. As it is desirable to be able to hang trophies at will, I decided to place 1/2-inch plywood over the base of sheetrock, then nail and glue the 3/4 lumber over the plywood — making a total of an inch and a quarter of solid wood to hold a nail for a head hanger. This much wood will suffice for all but the largest of trophies, such as elk, moose, cape buffalo etc. For these larger heads I feel that the hanging nail or screw should be secured to a stud. My wall is sheeted with blue stained, wormy ponderosa pine, 1 x 6 lumber. The proper angle to cut each board had to be calculated. Once determined, it was easy to maintain with a radial arm saw. Glen Hacker advised me that if I used paneling adhesive as well as nails, I could use random length boards. Using this system you do not need to break joints on a stud.

Wall with pine lumber installed diagonally.

As a fire prevention measure, sheetrock should be installed under plywood. The advantage of following the random length system is that your eye will not notice any particular line of joints. The human brain will only take in the overall effect of the wall. I cannot be considered anything but a hobby carpenter, and I had no trouble whatever in constructing this wall.

I tried to create a different effect on one wall of my African room. I was attempting to establish the feeling that one was looking at a stuccoed wall in an overseas country estate. To a box of pre-mixed plaster, I added a generous portion of fine white sand, then smeared it over the sheetrock with a trowel, leaving a rather rough texture. The end result has not been painted. Even a beginning builder should have no trouble doing this and the material cost is minimal.

Another very pleasing and inexpensive wall covering is burlap. It can be pasted directly over sheetrock. It is so easy to install that most anyone should be able to hang it. Ordinary burlap fabric is usually a light brown, which provides a nice neutral color.

Rooms set aside exclusively for big game trophies will normally have high walls and will require a great amount of light to properly show off heads to their fullest. Sometimes you may want to accent certain trophies, and on other occasions you may want to leave some of your heads inconspicuously in the background. Zone lighting should certainly be considered as an ideal way to illuminate your trophy room.

My 20 by 32 African trophy room, with no windows and a 17 foot maximum wall height, has a total of 17 overhead light fixtures. As I enter the doorway I have six lighting switches at my command. One controls the general lighting, which consists of three fixtures, each with a 150-watt decorator bulb. The general lighting zone gives enough illumination so that everything in the room can be seen and enjoyed. In addition there is a switch to control each of the four zones. A zone includes up to four flood lights covering a quarter of the room. For example, my fish collection is lighted by one zone with four flood lights. The sixth zone activates one side of a wall outlet, to which I have plugged my stereo system. All I have to do is throw the switch and the visitor to my room will hear authentic African drum music, maybe the bugling of a bull elk, or even the screams of a troop of baboons being harassed by a leopard. I think the effect is most pleasing.

Wiring this zone system was well beyond my abilities, but my electrician friend, Russ Moody. was able to complete the project in part of an afternoon.

If there is anything I hate to see in a room or building of rustic decor, it is the use of modern nails. Barn boards are often used as a wall covering and held in place with a newly manufactured bright nail. Why I don't know, for old-fashioned type hand cut nails are not difficult to find and

A simple wall coating of plaster and sand over sheetrock.

don't cost that much. There are several suppliers of hand cut nails who provide catalogs. The one that I have dealt with is The Company Store, PO Box 111, Wareham, MA 02571.

Depending upon the size and cut desired, they cost approximately $2 per pound. Some are colored black and those that are bright can be easily antiqued by placing them in a container filled with soil and water. Iodine and water will also do the trick.

The Company Store also offers rustic door fixtures in their catalog.

I use these hand cut nails for building doors, nailing barn boards in place, for trophy hangers and as decorative hangers for various collectables.

One time while visiting Jack Atcheson's Taxidermy Studio at Butte, Montana, I noticed that the concrete steps leading to the front door were crisscrossed with tracks of various exotic big game animals. I liked the idea, so have applied the concept several times myself. You do need some animal feet to start with. One can easily save feet from big game by either drying them or by placing them in a freezer. Drying may not be satisfactory in a damp climate.

When we poured the floor for my African trophy room, some concrete was left over. The truck dumped it in front of where the doorway was to be. With a hoe, it was smoothed into an irregular shape with a few flat rocks positioned in place. Between the rocks I formed tracks using the feet from several animals including deer, impala, nyala, mountain goat and

A beautiful trophy room belonging to Vern Wilson of Hamilton, New Zealand.

zebra. My African room is a split level with a foot elevation difference between the two floors. I poured a single long step between the two levels, which was also covered with animal tracks. To make them more prominent I painted the tracks a bright red.

So often one can look past the primitive beauty of ill fitting, weather-beaten boards to the ugly shine of foil-backed insulation. Why? The builder has used little foresight in planning his wall that should be an object of admiration and beauty. One should always assume that barn boards will be ill fitting and that they will shrink. The easiest solution to minimize the appearance of cracks is to place tar paper under the boards. Other builders use black paint on the insulation behind each potential crack.

Another very attractive wall decoration is the use of fish netting, either new or used. It makes an interesting wall in its own right, or as a background for a mounted fish collection. One can let his imagination run wild. First I nail a series of unequally spaced brads or picture hangers near the top of the wall for net hangers. As you place the netting, remember to drape it in bunches. If it is stretched evenly over the wall much of the effect is lost. Try to end up with sags, loosely draped bunches of net, combined with tightly stretched areas. This is the base to which you can add the frosting. You can attach with light leader material all manner of interesting objects, such as seaweed, clam shells, crab shells, star fish, dried shrimps, sand dollars and hopefully a few mounted fish.

Another novel decoration that is seldom seen in trophy rooms is the use of dead bird mounts. They can be hung on leather throngs giving the illusion that the birds are being hung for aging. If your wife approves of the display they can really add to the beauty of your kitchen.

Chapter Nine

SHORT COURSE ON MOUNTAIN GOAT HUNTING

Recently I needed to leave a friend, who had no previous alpine experience, on his own for several days of mountain goat hunting. Because of high winds I was unable to return with my plane. Besides, another friend needed my help in fixing his dinged up airplane. As I prepared to leave Tom, I began reeling off rules on goat hunting in quick order. Some he retained, some confused him and some he forgot. This experience with Tom prompted me to draft a series of rules for the hunting of many of the species of big game. Hopefully, you may avoid some of the pitfalls that have plagued me in the past. These rules are mine and the concepts have worked for me in the taking of an even 20 mountain goats, plus about 40 more for clients.

1. Never climb unless you have your quarry spotted. Glassing can usually be readily done from below. The hunter who climbs on speculation will usually have a tired body, but not much else for his efforts. If you use a horse, this rule is not so important.

2. In coastal environments, ascend through the timber. That brush that looks so easy from a distance is a jungle of the first order.

3. Unless you are in good physical condition stay away from the coastal environments. I think that you will find non-coastal habitats, where horses can be used to gain elevation, much easier to hunt. You are much less likely to be rained out of non-coastal areas. On the other hand, coastal country may harbor the largest goat herds and they may be lower in elevation.

Montana billy. Photo by Paul Johnson.

4. Don't shoot at a running goat unless he is about to escape over the hill. Normally he will stop and provide you with a standing shot. If you startle a mountain goat at 200 yards you will probably be able to fire a box of shells at him before he reaches 400 yards — all standing shots.

5. Do not shoot unless you are certain that your trophy can be recovered. If he falls into oblivion, or an inaccessible gully,   what was the sense of the kill? It was a waste.

6. If the goat is standing in terrain that you cannot climb to recover his carcass, do not shoot until he moves to terrain where he will roll to recoverable country.

7. WATCH WHAT YOU ARE CLIMBING! It is much easier to ascend than to descend. More than one neophyte goat hunter has gotten himself into trouble here. Chasing mountain goats can be the most dangerous hunting in the world. Many a hunter new to the alpine doesn't realize that the upward climb is much easier than the return. A mountain sheep can travel in almost impossible habitat. A mountain goat can thrive in terrain where a sheep would never make it. He can live in country where no human can follow. DO NOT FORGET; YOU CANNOT FOLLOW A MOUNTAIN GOAT.

8. In timbered mountain goat habitat like you will find in Montana or Idaho, be out hunting early as they bed in the trees during mid- day.

9. Mountain goats generally lie down from about ten in the morning until four in the afternoon. It is easier to plan a stalk if you feel that your target is going to remain put.

10. Nannies and young billies are excellent eating in spite of what you may have read. About 50 percent of the old bills will be so tough as to defy description. The flavor will be excellent however.

11. Forget all those crazy rules you have heard about holding high or low if you are shooting uphill or downhill. ALL THAT COUNTS IS HORIZONTAL DISTANCE. Bullets are affected by gravity as are all other free-falling objects. Newton's laws of gravity explain it all: $d = 1/2 \, gt(2)$ or distance of fall equals $1/2$ (32) X time in seconds squared. No matter; if you are shooting up or down, only horizontal distance counts. If you are shooting up a steep slope and the target is 350 yards away, but only 200 horizontal yards; hold for a 200 yard shot.

12. Never hold over on your first shot. Low shots are easier to spot than high ones. Eighty percent of all hunters hold too high. Your target may be closer than you think. A 270 sighted in to be three inches high at 100 yards will be only 10 inches low at 400 and 27 inches low at 500, which is a long ways.

13. Protect your feet. If you wear cotton socks next to your feet and wool over them, you should never develop blisters. Blisters can ruin a hunt, and has for many hunters. By following this rule I have not had injured feet in years.

The age can be told by the rings.

Author's 1985 Montana mountain goat.

Richard Sawaske of Fresno, California, with a 10 1/8 inch billy he took in the East Kootenays of British Columbia. Photo courtesy Richard Sawaske.

14. Do not get caught on top overnight without your tent and sleeping bag. Almost every year some hapless mountain goat hunter perishes from exposure.

15. Once the hunter is on top, the goat does not know how to cope with you. It is against his instincts to descend, but once in a while he will surprise you.

16. In the "North" mountain goats will lay on snow or glacial ice during the heat of day, if it happens to be warm. I often plan my stalks so as to head towards snow. In the southern habitats they escape the heat by bedding in the timber.

17. Uphill or crosshill stalks are not as difficult to execute and complete as many would have you believe.

18. I have scored on several goats by shooting into the air. The report has brought them to their feet when nothing was showing moments before. A shot or rolled rock may also send them climbing to you, if you are on top.

19. In the northern coastal environments, goats will descend to winter range with fall's first snows. I have shot many by not climbing at all. They will nearly always stay where there is a cliff at their back.

20. Never hunt mountain goats alone. What would happen if you were injured with no one to help you? You could easily perish as the result of a minor injury.

21. Crampons and ice axes can be great aids in climbing, but they will lead you into terrain that you can't descend. I believe these tools should be left to the experts.

22. Getting caught on top overnight could cost you your life or at best great discomfort. I always allow as much daylight for the downhill return as I did for the ascent. Usually the return takes 60 percent as long as the climb, but it may take longer. A heavy load of meat may slow you down. You may need to use a new route, or you may suffer from a blister. Getting slightly lost is not impossible.

23. Sometimes a goat may hang up. If after five minutes it does not roll free fire another shot. The impact may relax its muscles, allowing the carcass to start rolling again.

A grizzly bear.

Chapter Ten

SHORT COURSE ON BEAR HUNTING

On the following pages I have attempted, in a concise form, to abbreviate the rules I follow when pursuing the bruin. This knowledge has been gained while taking, or assisting in taking while guiding, approximately 150 bears of all species.

1. Eyesight. All bears have very small eyes and poor vision. Even at 50 yards he seems to have trouble telling what you are unless you are skylined. Some will disagree, but I have found this to be true in my experiences.

2. Hearing. I believe that bears can hear no better than a human, or not much better. A noisy hunter will seldom fool Mr. Bruin.

3. Smell. Bears have an amazing sense of smell. Your scent, or lack of it, is of number one importance in collecting a trophy.

4. Sit. Once you have found a major feeding area sit, sit and sit some more. The walking bear hunter seldom collects his prize.

5. Do not walk through the area you intend to hunt. Approach your stand from the fringes. Human scent will drive a bear from his feeding grounds. This is probably the most common mistake made in bear hunting. I have watched bears spook from my track that was many hours old. Remember, stay out of the bear's actual feeding areas.

6. In all western U.S. and Alaska areas that I am familiar with, evening hunting is much more productive than early morning hunting. I don't know why this is true, but most guides will verify this statement. One outfitter told me that 22 out of 23 bruins taken from his camp last spring were shot during the afternoon hours.

7. Spring hides may be of higher quality than early fall pelts, but many spring hides will be rubbed; i.e. patches of guard hair will be missing.

8. When on a proper diet, bear meat can be excellent eating. I often have the hams and shoulders smoked. When thus treated it tastes close to pork.

9. When hunting in the mountains, remember drainage winds tend to flow down valley morning and night and upvalley during the day.

10. Squaring the hide. To square a hide, lay it out like a rug and the squared measure will be the average of the length (tip of nose to tip of tail) and the width (claw tip to claw tip).
   A. A small black will square four feet. An average black will square five to six feet. Anything over seven feet is huge.
   B. Few grizzly hides will square over seven and half feet. Most will be in the six to seven foot range.
   C. On the giant Alaskan browns few will square over nine feet. I and most other guides feel a hunter should take a hard look at anything approaching eight feet. Those monster tens are virtually a legend.

11. There is no real difference in appearance between the Alaskan brown and the grizzly. Taxonomists classify them all as Ursus arctos.

Author with a huge Alaskan brown bear from Afognak Island.

12. How can you tell the black bear from the grizzly in the field?

A. Black bears have short (2 1/2 inches or less) sharply curving claws, while grizzlies have longer (over three inches) straighter claws. If you can see the claws at a distance it is a grizzly for they are more massive than on a black.

B. Black bears do not have pronounced humps; grizzlies may or may not. If you see a hump it is a grizzly.

C. Color is no criteria as all colors will and do appear in both species, but only the grizzly/ brown will be silver tipped or grizzled.

D. The ears are a giveaway. Black bears ears are much more pronounced than on a grizzly, which look like little rounded knobs. This is my main criteria for telling the two species apart.

E. The grizzly has a dished face, while the black bear has a straight profile.

13. The shoulder shot is the surest stopper of a bruin. With one shoulder broken he can't run in a straight line. With both shoulders smashed, he is down. I try to hit from 1/4 to 1/3 of the way up from the bottom of the body.

14. Bears are poor bleeders because of their dense underfur and thick coat of lard and fat. Often there will be no blood trail at all, even with a fatal hit. I have found that you need to use at least a 32 caliber (8mm) to be reasonably certain of external blood flow.

15. Bears often violently react to a superficial hit. He may fall as though mortally wounded, when only hit in the paw.

16. When hunting open areas, additional terrain can often be viewed by climbing a tree. This is my normal means of hunting when pursuing bruins on the coast of Alaska.

17. I try to hunt prime habitat only. I have found in Montana that many hunters spend their time in areas that are too dry. Bears are like people; they like succulent food associated with damp areas.

18. If under intense pressure, bruins tend to only come out to feed in open areas after dark. Heavily hunted and trophy bears usually feed in the smaller openings. Seldom will you see a bruin in the middle of a large opening; if you do he is probably an immature animal. WATCH THE EDGES.

19. I have found that if you need binoculars to tell if it is a bear, it isn't.

20. When skinning you only need to save the front foot pads when mounting a life-size with one or more front feet raised. The rear pads never need to be kept.

21. Bears do not occur in densities like hooved animals. Grizzlies will seldom occur, over their range, in numbers exceeding one per 20 square miles. Seasonally he may be found in densities as great as one per square mile. On the better habitats along the coast of Alaska, brownies sometimes live in densities exceeding one per square mile, which would be considered a high black bear density.

22. Any bear hide up to eight feet square in size, complete with skull, can be easily packed out over your shoulders. A bruin over this size will require a pack frame to be carried very far. A very large well fleshed Alaskan brown bear pelt may exceed 150 pounds in weight.

23. You can approximate the size of the hide by measuring the width of the front foot in inches, add one and that will be the size of the bear pelt in feet.

John Haubauer and his large Alaska Gulf coast brownie.

Chapter Eleven

SHORT COURSE ON MULE DEER HUNTING

Since first hunting mule deer during a fall hunt in the state of Wyoming, it has become one of my favorite animals. The hunter can work as hard as he wishes for his buck, depending upon the habitat he chooses to chase his quarry in. For many a meat hunter he is the animal that fills the larder with little effort, while he can be frustration first class to the serious trophy hunter. For the past decade I have spent more mandays after trophy muley bucks than any other animal. The short course that follows pertains mainly to the collection of mountable mule deer bucks.

1. The mule deer may live in a greater diversity of habitats than any other large mammal in the world. He is found from the sub-arctic taiga of the Canadian provinces to the semi-deserts of central Mexico. Without a doubt, more trophy mule deer are killed from mountainous habitats than any other. Most of our truly wild lands, that are but little trod by man, are in the high country. Mule deer by nature are open country animals, so don't expect to find deer in large numbers in heavily timbered mountains. In the southern Rockies, many of the mountain ranges are typically open hillsides interspersed with aspen and conifer patches.

2. Muleys are found throughout the timber lands of the West, from the boreal spruce timberlands of northern Canada southward to the dry oak and chaparral forest of southern California and Mexico. Most of their time is spent in the fringes, as dense forest and mule deer don't go together. The more thinly forested lands of the river breaks are my favorite haunts of the mule deer. Here the habitat is prime, with high population numbers.

Author's son, Stuart, killed this mature muley buck on a central Montana hunt.

3. Some of the highest mule deer densities are found in the plains of eastern Montana, Wyoming and the western Dakotas. On casual observation one would not think that a deer could hide in such country, but cover there is. The erosion courses, which are locally called coulees, are favorite sites of muley hunters. Coulees can be anywhere from a few feet deep to elevation differences of as much as 500 feet, as are the Missouri Breaks. Here the species feels secure from predators, including man.

4. The desert of the American southwest, and on into Mexico, is also the home of the muley, including the desert and burro varieties. I have not hunted him in this environment, but I understand he is usually only found in low numbers, and is quite difficult to locate. Tracking is a common method of the more successful hunters. Extreme desert areas do not provide habitat for the deer as there is nothing to eat.

5. When a hunter studies the Boone and Crockett Record Book it is obvious that most of the truly large muleys come from Colorado. Of the top 50 typicals listed in the 1981 "Book," 25 came from this state. The number drops to 12 of 50 top non-typicals. It would seem obvious that Colorado is the state to hunt. Is it? I once asked the noted hunting consultant Jack Atcheson where I should go to collect an outsized muley buck.

Jack surprised me with his answer. "Why leave your own state of Montana? Maybe Montana doesn't have many deer listed in the record book, but right now your chances as an individual hunter are probably better in collecting a mounter than in any other state. Colorado has so much pressure the odds of killing a big one are close to nil." Today, several years later, I have come to appreciate these words. Next to Colorado, New Mexico has the most in the top 50 with seven, followed by Wyoming with six, Utah five, Idaho three and Arizona and Oregon each with two. In the decade and a half I have been chasing the species, I have been involved with two animals that nearly made the "Book," one from central Idaho and the other from western Montana. Instead of looking at states, I think one should consider individual areas that are producing quality heads now.

A large mule deer shot by the author on a 1983 hunt to central Montana. This buck was killed 200 yards from a main gravel road.

6. What is a good muley? That is the question today's mule deer hunter must ask himself. Each of us must set our own standards. Twenty years ago when I first started pursuing the species, most head hunters felt they needed to find a buck with a 27-inch outside spread. The standard of superiority has been a 30-inch spread. The minimum Boone and Crockett score needed to win a permanent place in the "Book" is 195 points. Today, a 170 point buck is excellent in most places and 145 is considered a mounter by most. Few hunters will turn down a head with a 23 inch spread, as long as it sports the typical 4 by 4 conformation. A head tallying the minimum 130 Safari Club International points needed for their book makes a nice mounter, but not a super head.

7. When judging muley bucks, most hunters think mainly in terms of outside spread. Outside spread does not even count as a measurement for the "Book". If the inside spread exceeds the length of the longest beam there is a deduction in score. A buck's ears when spread straight measure 21-22 inches. If the antlers extend two or three inches beyond the ears you are looking at something approaching the 30-inch class. Typically, a mature buck will have four points per side plus a brow tine. The four points look like two pairs of Y's. If you don't see the Y's then you are not looking at a 4 by 4. The Y's can be verified even if you can barely see the antlers. You don't need to count points. Look for deep Y's. This indicates long points. Shallow Y's will have short points and won't add up to much score.

The Boone and Crockett system stresses symmetry, while the Safari Club system only recognizes total mass. With mule deer, I think I favor the SCI method of scoring.

A giant set of typical mule deer antlers that was killed by Leland Crow of Hamilton, Montana. This buck was killed in the Bitterroot Valley, which is an area that does not produce many mule deer.

8. What does it take to produce a big mule deer buck? Unless the proper genetic make up is present a set of super antlers will never be produced. It is the same with humans; some families tend to produce larger offspring. A family of runts is not likely to beget any seven-foot-tall basketball players.

Given the best genetics possible, bucks will still not produce outstanding antlers unless there is enough food, rich enough in nutrients, to produce bountiful antler mass. High density deer populations tend to deplete the soil of nutrients, so populations with large numbers of animals tend to produce smaller animals with small headgear. I am told such was the case during the peak years in New Zealand. Low animal numbers on a range, compared to the carrying capacity, favor the production of top trophies. In the part of Montana where I live there are few muleys found, and yet, some outstanding trophies are periodically taken. In 1983 a New Zealand hunter collected an exceptional buck in our valley, with a green score of 217 6/8. Number two listed in the 1981 "Book" has a score of 217. There are so few muleys locally that I don't think any serious trophy mule deer hunter would ever come to the Bitterroot. As the antlers have left the U.S. it is doubtful if this rack will ever be officially scored.

Unless a buck can live long enough to grow to maturity, no matter what else, the hunter just isn't going to put that big rack on the wall. Easily hunted habitat with good access is a poor place to be looking for a trophy, especially with the current interest in hunting big bucks. The wall hangers will be found in remote areas far from roads, areas that are seldom hunted because of the terrain, private land with limited accessibility, or areas with a limited number of permits.

9. The area must be huntable. In section 8, I noted a huge buck with a green score of 217 that was killed near my house. I seldom hunt in areas close to home because I do not consider the terrain huntable. Much of the high country in the Bitterroot is so dense when one does see a deer it will probably take imagination to figure out what one is looking at. One might try for days before seeing anything, then when game is spotted you won't be able to determine size. By comparison, in the semi-open, subalpine or breaks type habitats generally one can get a good look at most anything that is flushed, along with being able to study many bucks from afar with a spotting scope.

10. For those that have the time, and or money, hunting way back in a designated wilderness area, via horseback, is probably the most satisfying both from the killing standpoint and in regard to having a totally satisfying experience. One should remember that good mule deer hunting and good elk hunting seldom occur in the same locale.

11. One does not normally think in terms of quality trophy hunting near roads, but during the fall migration to winter range, and during the rut, trophy bucks can often be found near roads. I have found in the relatively open habitats of eastern Montana, where it is easy to see deer from a vehicle, that most hunters refuse to walk. Often just a half mile from a 4-WD drive track one can find much better trophy hunting than he can experience by staying with his 4-WD. I commonly see 10 4 by 4's per day by walking just beyond most of the deer hunters.

12. Areas with limited permits have great potential for finding an outstanding trophy. Arizona, as well as several other states, have such areas. If you are lucky enough to draw you should score on a mounter.

13. If you can find private property that has a mule deer population with a limited amount of hunters allowed on the premises, your chances of scoring on an older buck will increase. The key is, a portion of the bucks need to have an opportunity of living to old age. In simple words this means light hunting pressure.

14. Most hunters on foot will not shoot an animal they feel that they cannot drag out. There is an easier way. We remove the front shoulders, plus hams, bone the rest, and then pack it out on a frame.

Last fall we weighed the meat from a mature buck so treated — 117 pounds. Gordon Michens, a local butcher with considerable experience as a hunter, reports that the large muley buck he killed last season yielded 105 pounds of boneless meat. The live weight was estimated at 280.

Gordon says in butchering hundreds of game animals he has found the following: There is a 40 percent weight loss in gutting, skinning, removal of head feet and in trimming away fat. There is a further 25 percent reduction in weight in the boning process. He says in actual practice, by the time you trim away bloodshot meat, the meat yield approximates 1/3 of the original live weight. Even the largest of muley bucks should be an easy pack in two loads.

15. Prime time is just that — the daylight hours when game is most active. The duration of good huntable time is controlled by weather and amount of darkness. In periods of warm, clear weather, with a full moon the hunter may have less than 1/2 hour to see deer in numbers, each morning and night. If temperatures are down to 10 above, a storm brewing and the moon just a splinter the hunter may have a full three hours, morning and night, of productive time.

16. Pending storms and cold weather seem to make deer much more active. When night time temperatures plunge below zero it takes a lot of food to keep a large animal going. Last season when chill factors dipped to 70 below in eastern Montana, deer were active nearly all day. During a storm deer tend to stick close to cover which makes conditions tough for the glasser, but may also help the serious still hunter.

17. Planning a muley hunt around the proper phase of the moon can be quite rewarding. On moonlit nights, deer will be feeding most of the night and will head for cover soon after first light. During the new moon or cloudy skies, game will tend to feed much later in the morning and will be active earlier in the afternoon.

18. Without binoculars and spotting scope, the mule deer hunter is seriously hampering himself. Deer beyond 600 yards can become almost an impossibility to see with the naked eye. Without a spotting scope, the hunter will waste much time pursuing bucks that are not worthy of stalking. One day last fall I located over 100 deer from a single vantage spot, where minutes before a group of hunters had said there wasn't a deer in the country. They were not glassing. Binoculars and the ability to use them is the number one way of seeing more game.

19. As most mule deer are shot at longish range, a flat shooting, high velocity rifle is a must. As deer are neither especially tough or dangerous, I prefer to stay away from heavy recoiling rifles. I have killed most of my muleys with a 270 Winchester, but have also downed quite a few using the 257 Roberts with hot handloads. Although I don't own one, I think the 7mm Magnum is a fine choice. The 243 and 6mm are also decent choices as they shoot flat, but they might be a bit on the light side.

A buck any hunter would be proud of. Photo by Larry Hilton.

A large set of Montana muley antlers in the L.V. Crow collection. This set has too many deductions to score well as either a typical or nontypical, but it does have a three-and-a-half-foot spread.

20. Maybe one of the best ways for the serious trophy muley hunter to collect a good set of antlers is to find a pocket that has food, shelter and water and yet is far from the eyes of most hunters. Such country is typified by a mountain bowl with an alpine meadow, studded with pockets of fir and lying far above the dense timber of the lower slopes. Here one will find few deer, but there are some super bucks.

21. When mule deer are concentrated near country I can hunt from a vehicle, during the prime hunting hours I quickly drive from vantage point to vantage point using my binoculars and spotting scope. In as short a time as possible I can look at a great many acres. Hunting in this fashion, I have seen as many as 20 mature bucks in two hours and 100 deer from a single location.

22. I have noted over the years that when hunting from roads most hunters will choose through-routes rather than dead-end roads, as most people don't seem to want to back track. Because of the reduced pressure, I normally see more game from these dead-end roads. This is simply a case of doing what the average man doesn't.

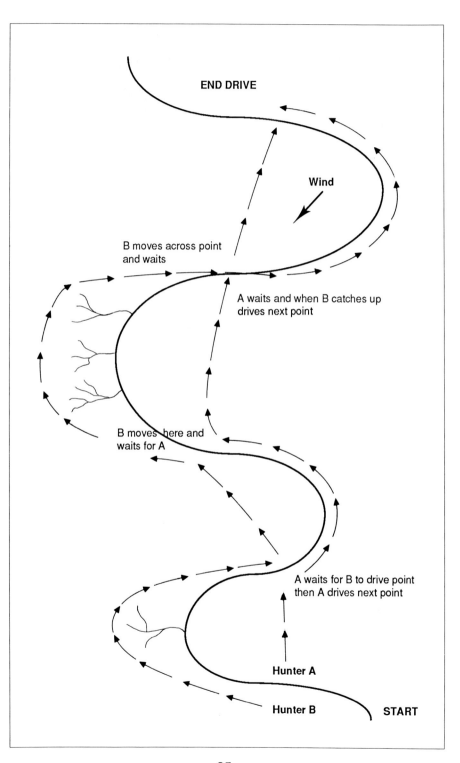

END DRIVE

Wind

B moves across point
and waits

A waits and when B catches up
drives next point

B moves here and
waits for A

A waits for B to drive point
then A drives next point

Hunter A

Hunter B

START

23. Hunting during the rut improves the hunter's chances tremendously. Bucks are on the move and only have sex on their mind. A big trophy can be found at any time of the day. About half the bucks I see during the rut are alone, indicating that they are looking for a receptive doe. In Montana and Idaho, I can be certain of the rut being active by November 8. I plan hunts accordingly. Many hunters, especially nonresidents, seem to hunt early in the season, especially the opening week. If they waited for the rut, their results might improve dramatically. Last fall I saw 15 mature muley bucks in a little over two hours on one occasion. The rut was in full swing.

24. Tracking is the primary method of many successful hunters in the snow country of the North, as well as for those that live in low deer density environments of the desert. It is a surprise to many that game can be trailed on bare ground, but it is much easier than imagined especially if you are working after a rain when fresh sign is obvious. An experienced bare ground tracker can trail almost as fast as he can walk. Without the clutter of leaves and needles sign is quite distinct.

25. In some mountainous areas, many bucks don't travel to lower elevations for the rut. The does either work upwards to the bucks or they don't breed. Only after the winter's snows accumulate to a man's waist will the old-time bucks think of descending to the low country. This is the kind of habitat where the dedicated hunter might score big.

26. If you will inspect the color of mule deer antlers, many of the larger sets will be a dark brown in color, while a majority of smaller ones will have a grayish cast. The antler color is imparted from whatever the deer rubs his velvet on. If this is a sagebrush deer his horns will be light in color, and his life will probably be short, as he lives in habitat that makes him highly vulnerable to the hunter's bullet. In our state, the dark brown coloration is imparted from rubbing on juniper bushes, which is some of the thickest, nastiest deer habitat one can hunt. It should be apparent that many of the big old-timers live near juniper bushes. Once one has hunted this type of vegetation, it is easy to understand how a buck can live to the ancient years.

27. In eastern Montana and Wyoming, one seldom sees hunters trying to walk the coulees which are ravines cut by erosion. They seldom have water in them during the hunting season. They are almost impossible for the single hunter to hunt effectively. There are just too many escape routes for a smart old buck. Ambitious hunters often use the two- or three-man drive, which I call the Point System. The phrase comes from the fact that one hunter is walking directly across a bend (a point) in the coulee. Hunters that can work well together will see many bucks that most would never find. The hunter on the inside of the bend cuts across the point and waits for the second hunter to walk the outside. This man should always be able to see the coulee bottom. Once he catches up, the appropriate person cuts across the next point. If there are three hunters the odd man walks the coulee bottom.

28. When hunting semi-open habitats where the hunter feels there is a buck bedded close by, he can often be brought to his feet with a predator or elk call. Blow the call to produce a strange sound; any kind of noise. Deer will often spring to their feet, and stare, giving the sportsman ample time to glass and shoot.

29. As I live in a state with bountiful mule deer, it is only natural that we have lots of muley meat in the freezer. We do not like it quite as well as elk, moose or whitetail, but it still provides good eating. Does are especially good, but the old trophy buck can be a bit on the chewy side, especially if the rut is on.

Trophy western Montana bucks. Photo courtesy Tom Cross and Larry Hilton.

Western Montana is blessed with many fine whitetails. Photo by Larry Hilton.

Chapter Twelve

SHORT COURSE ON WHITETAIL DEER HUNTING

The whitetail deer certainly leads as North America's most numerous and best loved big game animal. Having grown up in the populous East, my first big game hunt was for whitetail deer. After moving to Alaska, deer hunting opportunities shifted to the Sitka blacktail. I often traveled to Montana or Wyoming to hunt deer and antelope, after completing my guiding contracts in the 49th state. On these trips the bulk of my efforts were directed towards the mule deer. It has only been in recent times that my enthusiasm for the whitetail has risen to a fevered pitch. My adopted homestate of Montana does offer some of North America's greatest opportunities to collect a wall hanger whitetail. As I have killed but a handful of deer of this species, I have enlisted the help of others with more knowledge of the species than I. They include Jack Atcheson Sr., the internationally known hunting consultant; my good friend, Larry Hilton, who has collected numerous whitetails from throughout its range; and Ed Wolff of Stoney-Wolf Video, which is one of the major outdoor video producers. Ed has recently finished writing a book on hunting big whitetail deer bucks.

1. The whitetail is a most adaptive animal. It has thrived in the face of advancing civilization, while other species have declined. Throughout his range, he is found in a wide diversity of habitats, with but one common factor. He needs thick dense security. Over much of his range in the East, dense cover is easy to find, but in the more open West it is amazing how he utilizes what little is available for hiding.

Ed Wolff, author of the whitetail hunting book *Taking Big Bucks*, with a whitetail deer he took with a bow.

2. Deer are found in large numbers throughout the South and westward into Texas. Three decades ago deer were scarce throughout the region, but today, thanks to modern game management and changing agricultural practices, their numbers are almost limitless. Wolff says that changing agricultural practices have brought the deer of Alabama from extremely low numbers to such a population boom that a hunter can kill a buck a day during their long season. Texas has more total deer than any other state and also boasts a multi-deer limit. Much of the Lone Star State is hard to hunt brush land that requires vastly different hunting techniques from the more northern environments.

3. In the West the whitetail can be found in a multitude of habitats ranging from dense river bottom vegetation to brush patches surrounded by farmland. It is not unusual to see whitetail bucks in the relative open. The species will hide in brush so short that few hunters would suspect that it would hide a deer. The largest buck I ever laid eyes on was spooked from a half-acre patch of brush that was less than two feet high. There was no other cover for at least two miles in all directions. In parts of eastern Montana, large numbers of whitetails can be found in the open pine forest. Here one can commonly see 100 or more whitetails a day. The species is found at lower elevations than the muley in the western habitats, but his range is moving up all the time. I saw a buck two years ago that was nearly 3,000 feet above the valley floor. He is now common in the conifer forest of western Montana, eastern Washington and northern Idaho.

4. I was born and brought up in New England where the whitetail reigns supreme. In that part of the world he is found in a great diversity of habitats. Here deer seldom expose themselves in open areas during daylight hours. His bedding grounds are typically dense, swampy habitats. Feeding areas vary depending upon food supplies.

Farther west in the middle part of the country one finds more productive crop land interspersed with hardwood timberland. It is here that maybe the largest antlered whitetails live.

5. Trophy whitetail bucks seem to crop up from all over their range, but what is your chance as an individual in harvesting one. This is all that you are interested in. Texas has produced more "Book" bucks than any other state by a wide margin. As a drawback, hunting is mostly on a pay basis and is most expensive. Montana is producing excellent bucks and I feel that one's odds of collecting a respectable head are high. This is probably the sleeper state to hunt, as hunting pressure is minimal. Lately, the western Canadian provinces are producing some outstanding bucks, but guides are normally required. Northern Maine always seems to produce its share of nice trophies, but one does not see the large number of animals that one will in the West. The farm woodlots of the Midwest, with their ideal feed conditions coupled with minimal access, may be the nation's number one place to find that trophy of a lifetime. Lately some of the more serious whitetail hunters have been turning their attention to Old Mexico.

6. What is a trophy whitetail buck? Each hunter has his own standard. In parts of the East where pressure is heavy and success is low, any deer is considered a trophy. In many states in the East it is rare to find a buck older than 2 1/2. My good friend, Larry Hilton, feels that a serious trophy hunter should be looking for a buck that will score at least 130 Boone and Crockett points. Jack Atcheson, who deals with thousands of hunters each year, says that any 4 by 4, or larger, should be considered a trophy. Four by four antlers may be large or small, but they should all make a hunter happy who has not taken larger. To be listed in the "Book" a buck must score a minimum of 170 points. Taking one of this magnitude is a goal equal to winning a Vegas slot machine Million Dollar Jackpot.

7. Judging whitetail heads under average hunting conditions is an almost impossible task as one seldom has the opportunity to glass one, as he might many of the more open country species. To be considered a good trophy a buck should have at least 10 points in total, with an inside spread approaching 18 inches. In Montana an average buck will measure 16 1/2 inches from ear tip to ear tip. The points should be long giving the appearance of a high rack. As it takes 25 additional points to make the Book as a non-typical, a trophy should have close to 25 inches of extra point length.

Ed Wolff advises that the trophy hunter should keep in mind that on the average, 70 percent of the B & C score originates from main beam and point length, 18 percent from mass, and 12 percent from spread credit.

8. To grow trophy whitetail antlers the following conditions must be met:

A. The genetics must be such that the buck is capable of producing large antlers.

B. There must be an abundance of highly nutritious food such as one finds on the farmlands of the Midwest.

C. Bucks must have the potential to live long enough to grow trophy sized headgear. Somehow there must be minimal hunting pressure. If you can gain permission to hunt private land that is closed to most hunters and which has a population of undisturbed deer, then your odds of success rise rapidly.

9. In hunting many species I stress the importance of the area being huntable. An individual's chances of killing a trophy are better in an area that is open enough to glass than it is in the dense timber.

Wolff feels if you can find an area with trophy deer, no matter how thick the cover there is a hunting method that will prove successful. This may be true as the whitetail lives within a small home range.

10. Nearly all experienced hunters feel that it is important to be in the field at, or before, first light. Do not end your day's effort until the last rays of legal shooting light. The length of time that deer are active, morning and night, depends on many factors, such as phase of moon, temperature, and weather.

Many 170-point bucks are so clever that they never show themselves during daylight hours. As an example, the present world's record nontypical whitetail, which was a road kill in Missouri, was never seen by a human before he died.

11. The role of weather in deer hunting is most significant. Game tends to be highly active before and after a major storm. Still hunters generally prefer to be afield during bad weather as deer don't seem to be as spooky as usual. Glassers and trail watchers will not normally see much activity during a storm. Cold weather forces deer to become more active as their food requirements increase with a drop in temperature.

12. The phase of moon does have an effect on hunting. On clear, full moon nights game tends to eat all night, retreating to cover at the first sign of daylight, offering the hunter little prime time hunting. Some experts don't agree with this concept.

13. Any hunter who lives in a state with the whitetail season during the rut will testify that his chances of scoring increase during this time. Ed Wolff, who is originally from the South, feels that bucks do not grow nearly as careless in that part of the country, as they do in the West where he now lives.

All experienced Montana sportsmen that I consulted with on whitetail hunting agreed that the rut is the best part of the season to hunt. The hunter sees a lot more game as bucks are not nearly as wary, plus they are active most of the day. The hunter should be afield all day, and hopefully the buck of your dreams will make a mistake that will put his head on your wall.

14. Probably the very best way to hunt whitetails is from an elevated stand. Wolf explains the advantages this way:

A. The deer's eyes are taken away as he does not naturally look up.

B. You take his nose away for if you are upwind of him, scent will drift overhead. The deer has lost his most important protective advantage.

C. Lastly, as you are stationary you have taken the deer's ears away for you should be making no sound. The hunter can use his own ears to advantage as you will often hear game coming.

D. Sitting in hay stacks is a popular method in the West, and deer do not seem to notice you as long as you sit quietly. At a distance the hunter isn't at much of an angle from the deer's eyes, and yet a man is undetected. Why? I don't know but it works.

Elevated stands run the gamut from easy-to-climb trees to expensive manufactured rooms with numerous appointments to make sitting comfortable, if not luxurious. Most bowhunters rely on the elevated stand, and more rifle hunters should. A well placed stand can greatly enhance the odds of scoring on a drive. It is the method that Jack Atcheson suggests. I have only been a semi-serious whitetail hunter for a few seasons, but sitting in an elevated location is bringing me results.

The experts seem to agree that 10 feet is an ideal height to be above the ground. If hunting pressure from tree stands is intensive, maybe the hunter will have to climb as high as 14 feet.

Trial and error is often necessary to find the ideal location for sitting, especially for the archer. Rather than nailing steps to every tree in the forest most experts use screw-in steps, as they do not permanently leave a telltale blemish on the tree. In addition, another hunter can't climb into your stand. Many hunters carry portable stands, which allows for the ultimate in mobility.

Wolff notes that in areas where many hunters use elevated stands some deer learn to look up, but they appear to have trouble detecting the human if he remains still. Hunting from the elevated position is almost a necessity for successful hunting in the denser habitats of the country.

15. Rattling is a hunting method that originated in Texas. It has spread to other states; anywhere there is a season during the rut. It is a method that won't work unless certain conditions are met:

A. There needs to be a population with a large number of bucks, resulting in competition for does.

B. There has to be a large number of receptive does about. The system only works during the heat of the rut. It is a method that is only practiced with results by a few hunters. If there are lots of hunters afield, rattling might be a good way to get shot.

Wolff says the rattling hunter should set up near a scrape. He believes that unless bucks are of about the same antler size they will not fight. The man theorizes that does approaching a scrape can tell super bucks from inferior animals by the odor of the deer's scent.

Atcheson reports that he has seen curious bucks peering down bulldozer trails in Texas after someone has rattled. There are several books on the market that cover the method in detail.

16. Still hunting is the favorite method of many an expert deer hunter, including Ed Wolff. It is not a technique for the casual hunter as it is hard to apply. Most will scare deer out of the territory without getting a shot. One should not take a step forward until he is certain there is nothing in range.

17. Driving is commonly employed in the East, but is seldom practiced in the West. It works well where covers are small or where deer follow predicted routes. In New England driving is usually directed by the most experienced hunter. He specifies the routes drivers are to follow, as well as where the standers are to position themselves. I have enjoyed the system in eastern Montana, working the narrower covers along some of the river bottoms.

Atcheson says he has seen more whitetails taken by driving than any other method. I find the system most exciting as a stander. I am under the spell of intense anticipation when I think deer should be coming past my stand. It is a well-known fact that wise old bucks will often sneak past the drivers or may let a driver walk by, while he remains undetected.

Jack strongly believes that the most productive drives are conducted by paid drivers, who should work all covers no matter how dense and hard to penetrate. This is where the big boys will be bedded. Friends often find it all too easy to bypass the prime covers.

Deer must be kept moving, and most will leave their bedding grounds by the mere presence of a human. Noisy drives may be better and Atcheson has found unnatural sounds are best. He suggests carrying a coffee can filled with pebbles. In order to keep deer moving, Jim McIntyre, a deer hunting fanatic from Glasgow, Montana, says the beaters should walk fast giving game little opportunity to outflank them.

Atcheson believes that most large mammals have the ability to reason,

Internationally known hunting consultant Jack Atcheson with a trophy whitetail buck.

and he believes that a running deer doesn't think like a stationary animal. The standing deer can pick one of many options on how to escape his pursuer.

It is easier to push a deer from one security area to another than to attempt to drive him into the open.

Jack likes a combo of standers at narrow points in the cover, plus people sitting in tree blinds.

Ed Wolff avoids drives as he does not like to shoot at running bucks. Like Jack, he has found that most drivers will not work the denser cover.

We use the two man drive in the open type habitats found in eastern Montana, western Dakotas and Wyoming, where erosion courses locally called coulees harbor whitetails. The technique is the same as is found in section 27 of the previous chapter on mule deer hunting. The secret is that someone needs to have the coulee bottom in view at all times. Rock throwing is often in order. Many experts believe the method does not produce many large trophies.

18. Glassing as a technique is probably not conducted to the extent that it is with mule deer, as whitetail tend to live in denser habitat. The dedicated trophy whitetail hunter does carry glasses as he needs to pick apart brush to recognize deer parts. When sitting on a haystack, glasses help find bucks moving along the edge of fields in the dim light of late evening, or early morning. The elevated hunter can use glasses to great benefit in dense brush country.

19. In parts of Texas the cover is so thick that hunting by conventional methods is impossible. As hunting is on private land, baiting is commonly practiced. I have been told that corn feeders are often employed. In some areas deer respond to a known sound like a dinner bell, as they think they are going to be fed. In many circles this would not be considered as fair chase, while in other areas it is perfectly acceptable.

20. Tracking in the snow is a technique that is used with great results by a few hunters. Most fail miserably using the system. Many claim that you can't tell a buck from a doe track, and that you are just taking your chances following a large track. I believe most bucks tend to drag their feet in the snow. Maybe this isn't 100 percent, but it works most of the time. I killed my best whitetail by trailing in the snow. The majority of hunters do not have the skill or persistance to stay on a single spore, and soon give up. I have friends who claim they can walk a deer to the ground, and I am sure they can.

21. The flesh from whitetail deer should be considered as prime meat. Over parts of his range he has the benefit of eating prime agricultural crops, further enhancing the flavor of his flesh. If his meat, as with any wild game, receives proper field care then he will be excellent eating. You can't have dirty, improperly cooled flesh, covered with entrails and expect a taste treat. Field care must be done correctly.

Larry Hilton of Hamilton, Montana, with a large western Montana buck. Photo courtesy Larry Hilton.

Whitetail buck. Photo by Jim Bush.

22. Floating is an aesthetically pleasing and productive means of collecting a deer in many areas. Using a raft, canoe or small boat can yield access to country that is generally overlooked. Be certain that you aren't violating landowner rights or state laws before you take off on a deer hunting expedition by water. When approached by water, deer won't hear you coming. As you will be hunting areas with little pressure you should see lots of game. This is a little used method. Ed Wolff says he has floated with innertubes for deer in the Deep South most effectively.

23. Dogs are commonly used over much of the South where habitats are dense. If one thinks of the method, it is really a variation of driving with the dog replacing the man as a driver. Dogs are not legal for hunting deer over much of the country.

24. Today, the hardcore whitetail fanatic who wants nothing but the best spends most of the year looking for an outstanding buck to hunt during the season. Once located, the hunter will try every legal method at his disposal to collect his prize. As whitetails live on a limited home range this dedication to an individual animal often proves fruitful.

25. Rocking the draw is a method that will work in semi-open habitats with dense brush patches. Smart old whitetails have the habit of laying tight in cover that us humans hardly believe is fit to hide a rabbit. Pitching rocks will often bring a deer that would otherwise never have taken flight to its feet. Serious proponents of the system usually use slingshots or slings, such as David slew Goliath with. The local Boy Scout leader provided instructions for making my sling, and it is surprising how far and hard it will toss a rock.

Ed Shoemaker shot his best Coues' deer on a 1983 hunt to Arizona. It has an impressive B&C score of 104 points.

Chapter Thirteen

SHORT COURSE ON COUES' DEER HUNTING

The North American deer in his many forms is available to more hunters than any other genus. Each species is distinct in its appearance, home range preference and habits. One can scarcely pick up a sporting magazine without finding a how-to article on whitetails or mule deer. Books on either of these animals can be found by the dozen. When we think of lesser-known deer such as the Sitka blacktail and the Coues' deer, seldom do we find helpful information in print. Interest in the tiny desert whitetail, or Coues' deer, is growing rapidly. I have not hunted the animal myself but hope to in 1987. When I think of Coues' deer, all thought goes to my good friend, Ed Shoemaker of San Diego, California, a man with vast deer hunting experience. I enlisted his aid in putting together this chapter, as he is a man who is able to produce Coues' bucks.

1. The Coues' deer is found in the lower lying mountains of the American Southwest and portions of northern Mexico. Typically look for him on north slopes stocked with a dense stand of brush. He is not found on the flats, which seem reserved for the desert muley. In the eastern portion of his range he is found at higher elevations and on into the coniferous forest.

2. The species is found in portions of New Mexico, Arizona and Old Mexico. Nearly all "Book" entries are from Arizona, as most of his range is in that state. Ed feels there are no real hot spots, as his distribution is so restricted that the gene pool is nearly the same throughout his range.

3. What is a good Coues' deer? Shoemaker feels that a trophy head is anything scoring 80 B&C points. A mature rack will look like a small set of whitetail antlers and a "Book" set will have eight or more points including the main beam, with an inside spread pushing 15 inches. A large non-typical set needs at least 10 inches of total length of abnormal points, which means three or four extra tines. The minimum score for a record book typical is 110 with 120 for nontypical.

4. Judging heads of this species can be difficult, as you seldom get a chance to study your target. Even the very largest trophies are small, when compared to other subspecies of whitetail. Most shots are at running game. Ed advises that if the antlers appear massive you should shoot.

5. As with most big game species, Coues' deer are most active and more visible during times when they are feeding, which is during the first and last hour of daylight.

6. Like other deer, when it is storming the species tends to lay up, but actively feeds before and after inclement weather.

7. As with other deer, a full moon with clear skies encourages nocturnal feeding. Under these conditions deer tend to head for cover soon after first light.

8. Hunting during the rut, as with other species, gives the head hunter an edge. In Arizona there is a split season with the second segment occurring during the rut. Shoemaker notes that Coues' bucks do not get as goofy as males of other deer species.

9. Glassing is one of two primary methods of hunting the species. Ed warns do not look for him where you would expect to find mule deer as he won't be there. Coues' like to sun themselves on the points of ridges. They also bed under objects such as cactus. Many top trophy hunters use no other method. Shoemaker feels that the average hunter will have the best results using this technique, once he learns where to look.

10. The desire to lay under objects is a trait that can be turned against the species. Look for him at the base of rocks, cacti, etc., where he can see danger approaching. Remember he is nearly always found in dense brush that is six to 12 feet high.

11. Another way to hunt this animal of the deep brush is to walk, or ride, the ridges and toss rocks in an attempt to spook a buck into running. The decision to shoot or not to shoot, will have to be made rapidly, for he will be in full flight. One of Arizona's top Coues' deer guides uses this method exclusively. Slings and slingshots can aid the hunter.

12. Shoemaker feels that one can achieve a limited amount of success still hunting. He uses the method during the middle of the day when there isn't much else to do anyway.

13. Field care in the heat is not the problem one would think. During Arizona's first season temperatures seldom get over 70. Frost is the norm during the second season.

14. The Coues' deer is a small animal and it will take an exceptional animal to field dress over 100 pounds. Shoemaker says his best trophy weighed 102 pounds gutted. Two other bucks weighed 86 and 67 pounds.

15. As a meat animal he is good eating, as are most whitetails.

16. A good portion of Arizona's Coues' deer range is public land, so the nonresident will experience little trouble in finding a spot to hunt. Only a small portion of the species range is in New Mexico. Old Mexico is just beginning to gain some recognition as a place to hunt. It is suggested that the sportsman who plans one hunt only hire a guide. Coues' guides are inexpensive and a thousand dollars should be considered a high end price. If you don't hire a guide, figure on taking a year or so to learn the ropes. Ed says it took him three years to be a good trophy Coues' deer hunter.

Harry Johnson packing a Chistochina River moose.

Chapter Fourteen

SHORT COURSE ON MOOSE HUNTING

My friends know that in the world of hunting I love it all. My only negative thoughts about big game revolve around packing a large animal on my back for long distances, such as I have experienced in moose hunting. I have taken 14 myself and have helped others on several dozen occasions. Once, while living in Haines, Alaska, I brought out seven in my plane in seven days. My back hurt, my plane was a bloody mess and not much money was put in my pocket. I killed my first in 1962, and last hunted the species when my wife drew a Montana tag in 1983. Over much of my adult life, the bull moose has represented a huge piece of tasty meat. I have never tried to dedicate time for a trophy bull, and have always shot what was in front of me. Today, the aches and pains of past moose hunts have receded from my memory. Now is my time to kill a big trophy bull.

1. The Boone and Crockett Club recognizes three subspecies of moose with the largest being the Alaska Yukon, which takes a minimum score of 224 points to earn a place in the "Book". Next in size is the Canada moose, which needs a score of 195 to be recorded. This subspecies is also found in Maine. The Shiras moose occurs in the western U.S., and is the smallest variety. It only needs 155 points to qualify as a record book trophy.

Most hunters look for wide, spreading antlers, but equally as important are massive, wide palms and brows. Most antlers with wide spreads tend to lay flat, while those that are cupped tend to be narrow. Shoot a wide spreading bull with heavy palms and well developed brows and you will have a high scoring trophy.

2. The Canada moose is considered to be found throughout Canada, except for the Yukon and the Northwest Territories, plus the states on Minnesota and Maine. The best trophies come from northwestern British Columbia. In the southern part of the western provinces, heads are generally small and are probably actually of the Shiras strain. Maine is producing some nice heads and the current state record scores 214 4/8 points, with a 62-inch spread. Maine's moose hunting has only been open, in modern times, since 1981. The 1981 B&C record book lists the number one head as scoring 238 5/8 points, with a 65 5/8 spread. It was killed in 1914 in Quebec.

3. The range of the Shiras moose includes all of the Rocky Mountain region south of Canada. The "Book" list more heads from Wyoming than any other state by a wide margin. The world's record was harvested in 1952 from Wyoming and scores 205 4/8 points. Its spread was only 53 inches. An examination of the 1981 record book did not reveal any Shiras moose with spreads reaching 60 inches.

4. For sheer mass of antler material, the Alaska/Yukon moose is the granddaddy of all the world's antlered animals. He is found throughout Alaska, the Yukon and the Northwest Territories. Traditionally the best heads have come from the Kenai and the Alaska Peninsulas of Alaska. In recent times, I understand, some nice trophies are coming from the upper end of the Alaska Peninsula and from the Yukon Territories. The 1981 "Book" only shows number 10 of the top 10 coming from anyplace other than Alaska. The top scoring trophy was killed near McGrath in 1978 by Ken Best with a score of 255 and a spread of 77 inches. Number two was taken in 1961 almost in sight of the the states's largest city, Anchorage. It scored 251 and also boast a spread exceeding 77 inches. Two are listed with spreads exceeding 80 inches.

5. A moose is not very smart. A degree of care is needed in completing a stalk but not much During the rut, I have found that bulls are downright stupid and have often walked right up to one and shot him.

6. If you want to know where to find a moose, it is around his primary foods, which consist of willow, birch and aspen in that order of preference. Willow is by far the preferred feed of moose and that is what I look for when moose hunting. Heavily browsed willow will be chewed off to be the size of a man's thumb. When Pat drew a Montana moose tag in 1983, we scouted, before the season, for willow. When the season opened we spent our time watching a single one-acre willow patch. It was a most productive location and it seemed as though a high percentage of the moose in her unit used this one willow patch, from time to time.

Montana bull moose. Photo by Paul Johnson.

7. Most hunters new to the game of moose hunting think of the animal being found around a lake filled with pond lillies. In the northern mountainous environments his more typical habitat is in the high country, sometimes almost almost as high as sheep. He can be seen as high as one can locate willows. Many a trophy bull has succumbed to the sheep hunters bullet. Think of willow and you can't be too far wrong.

8. Looking around lakes and rivers is what most moose hunters think of. When I lived in Alaska, my boat hunting friends saw far fewer moose than I located in the high country.

9. Never shoot a moose in water, for if you do a monumental task awaits you. This is a large animal that is difficult enough to handle on the ground let alone in the water. I have never made this mistake, but friends who have say they will never attempt the task a second time.

10. During the rut, bull moose are often called in by various methods. In the heavily-timbered portions of eastern Canada, I understand that they are commonly called in with homemade horns. In Alaska I have summoned bulls by pounding on logs with a stick. On one occasion we were surrounded by seven lovesick moose. I tried a bull moose recording in an electronic game caller in Alaska during the fall of 1984, with no success.

Bringing out a hindquarter of a Montana bull moose.

11. Much moose habitat is quite open, so one can often inspect more ground by climbing and looking from trees.

12. Consider the use of binoculars in most habitats a must. In semi-open country, a good man with glasses may see several times more animals than the man who does not use them.

13. In the days before 1974 airplanes were commonly used in Alaska to spot moose. Most hunters would not shoot a bull unless they could nearly taxi their airplane to it. Since 1974 it has been illegal to fly and hunt the same day in Alaska. I understand there is a limited amount of airplane hunting for moose in parts of Canada.

14. This is one animal that never seems to drop with one shot. I have only seen two killed with one shot.

15. A moose is a large animal, but I have never found that it takes an especially powerful rifle to down him. Thinking back, I have killed moose with the following weapons: 6mm Remington, 257 Roberts, 264 Winchester Magnum, 270, 270 Weatherby, 300 Weatherby, 8mm Mauser and a 375 H&H. I also helped another fellow down a bull with a 44 Mag handgun. I took a friend out who easily dropped a meat moose with a 225. The 6mm and the 257 were on the light side and they should never be called adequate moose rounds. My favorite was the 8mm. If trophy hunting only I might be tempted to try shoulder shots, but as all my moose hunting was in the interest of meat I always made behind-the-shoulder lung shots. I have never lost a moose or ever even came close to having a problem. They just don't usually run off in a mad dash when wounded.

16. A moose is such a large animal that he must nearly always be cut into several pieces before he can be carried out. If packed out bones and all, it usually takes from six to eight loads. If the animal isn't going to be caped, remove the head first. When moose hunting I usually carry an axe or hatchet to help in butchering, but the entire job can be done with just a knife. Cutting off the head allows you to move him around much easier, especially if it is a bull. My butchering methods allow me to handle an animal of this size even when alone.

Once on the ground the animal may, or may not, be gutted, but it should be laying on its side. First I remove the front shoulder and then the ham, which can be laid on the hide if you don't have something else clean. If packing the meat very far and trying to keep the weight down, strip the backstrap from the carcass and bone the neck. The weight has now been reduced to the point that the carcass will be easy to roll onto the other side. Repeat the above operation. The only reason the hunter needs to gut a moose is to retrieve the tenderloins, which certainly are among the choicest cuts. Ribs can be packed out in their entirety or can be boned. Fresh barbecued moose ribs are fantastic but the fatty tissue will turn rancid if frozen, so we seldom freeze ribs. Moose liver is excellent, unless it is a bull in the rut, at which time it will be covered with white spots.

17. If you are going to have your moose mounted you must split the bell, otherwise it will spoil and fall off. Merely open the bell with a pocket knife then salt the flesh side. Not much to it really. Don't forget to complete the task, however, as a moose head looks mighty funny without a bell.

18. A moose is such a large animal that the skinner must take some extra precautions in caping. Salt will only penetrate 1/4 inch, so it is imperative that the nose be fully turned with all cartilage being removed. You might get away without completely turning a smaller big game animal's nose, but not the bull moose.

19. Next to wild sheep and goats, we enjoy eating moose meat better than any other wild game. We might even turn down prime beef for a good moose steak. My wife, Pat, is often asked how one should cook moose meat? The answer is simple, prepare it as you would beef. If the meat has been properly taken care of in the field it is a taste treat indeed. Bulls in the rut aren't quite as good, but even they aren't bad. One fact for certain, down a bull moose and you will be able to fill a good part of a freezer. A full round steak from a trophy sized bull moose is a cut of meat to behold. If you are fond of wild game, a moose won't last as long as you would think. With our large family, we can devour an entire critter in about 2 1/2 months.

To give you an idea of how big a moose is, we once removed a full hindquarter from a Yakutat bull and packed it 1 1/2 miles to the plane. It was later weighed in Juneau at 176 pounds. I actually carried it myself for 3/4 of a mile.

John Colclough and the author shot this moose in the Alaska Range over 20 years ago.

Chapter Fifteen

SHORT COURSE ON ELK HUNTING

Although I have killed eight elk and have been in on several others, I do not consider myself an expert on the subject of elk hunting. I have so many friends who are better, and more enthusiastic, elk hunters that I decided to draw on some of their experiences. I prefer to hunt mule deer over elk, and that must make me an oddball. For the fine points of elk hunting, knowledge was drawn from noted Montana sportsman, publisher, writer and video producer Dale Burk of Stonydale Press. Dale has participated on over a hundred bull kills as a hunter and guide. He is currently writing a book called *Confessions of an Elk Hunter.*

Bugling and archery techniques come from my friend, Larry Hilton of Hamilton, Montana, who is extremely successful in the game of elk hunting with a bow. Larry has been in on 39 five point or larger bull elk kills, covering several states. He has killed nine himself, including eight with a bow — with four scoring over 330 B&C points.

Maybe the dean of all elk hunters is internationally noted hunter, taxidermist and consultant Jack Atcheson Sr. He has killed an elk every year since he was 12 and he is over 50 now. Nearly all his elk have been large, trophy-sized bulls. Jack feels that he has been involved in about 200 kills of big bulls. I have seen what Jack and his sons shoot and most every season they bring in what to most hunters would be a trophy of a lifetime.

1. The elk is found in two totally different habitat types. One is the coastal forest of the Pacific Northwest typified by the rain forest of British Columbia, Washington, Oregon and northern California, with its towering giant Douglas fir trees and an understory of jungle-like ferns and mosses. To the north he is even found in the spruce forest of Alaska's Afognak Island. The other region comprises the Rocky Mountains and the adjoining ranges from Arizona and New Mexico northward to Alberta and British Columbia. He is even found in the North Woods of northern Michigan.

2. Timber and elk seem to be almost synonymous. Artists depict the lordly bull bugling in large spacious meadows, but how many are ever shot there? Most successful elk hunters find their quarry in the bottom of the deepest, darkest, most thickly timbered canyons in the area. Here the species feels secure. The Roosevelt elk of the coast considers his home the dense timberlands. Where there is any hunting pressure at all, even the Rocky Mountain elk spends the bulk of his time in the security of the heaviest timber possible. When it is cold, elk find it necessary to feed in open grassy meadows, or hillsides, but this is done at night. As soon as the gray of predawn begins to illuminate the skies they turn their noses towards cover and safety.

3. While most quality elk hunting takes place in mountainous terrain, few hunters think of looking for the species in the alpine far above sheltering trees that most of us assume is needed by the animal. I have seen large herd bulls with harems at 12,500 feet in Wyoming, a full mile from any tree growth. They are also found in this type of habitat in the state of Colorado.

4. When Lewis and Clark made their epic journey across the American West, the Rocky Mountain elk was a dweller of the plains. Here he was susceptible to the white man's rifle and was exterminated in less than a century, to remain only in inaccessible mountain valleys. Now that we are in the 1980's the elk can once again be found on the plains of portions of eastern Montana, in the vicinity of the Missouri Breaks. The Breaks are typified by deeply eroded water courses that are partly timbered with open, park-like stands of ponderosa pine. Here one sees elk bedded in open sagebrush during the middle of the day. This is hardly characteristic of elk that most of us know.

5. Where are the big trophies coming from? If the hunter should look at the 1981 edition of *Records of North American Big Game* he would find that 62 of 226 entries were killed in Montana or 27.4 percent. This is more than any other two states or provinces combined. Of the top 51 in the "Book," 11 were from Alberta, nine from Montana, eight from Colorado and Wyoming, and six from Idaho. No other place had more than two entries. For the small number of elk taken, Arizona is making an impressive showing of late.

The Roosevelt strain may have a larger body than the Rocky Mountain elk, but he is shy on headgear with the new number 1 scoring 384 3/8.

A trophy bull. Photo by Larry Hilton.

They are beautiful trophies, however, with their typically heavy mass and crowning. The best heads I believe are coming from Oregon. Afognak Island, Alaska, where I used to live, does not produce large antlers normally, although I did measure a six point shedder with a 51 1/2 inch beam.

6. What is a trophy bull elk? Every hunter has his own standard and today many consider a 5 by 5 or larger as worthy of collecting. Others think of a higher standard and would consider nothing less than the 6 by 6 as a suitable head. Serious trophy hunters in the West usually require that a bull carry six or more points per side, have 50-inch beams and score at least 300 B&C points. Entry into the record book requires 375 points.

Atcheson feels that over most of the elk's range a 5 by 5 should be considered a good trophy. He has this realistic advice to offer: "There may not be much difference between an average mature bull and a high scoring head, but there is a whole lot of difference between an average mature animal and no elk at all." He believes that a 5 by 5 should be compared to a 36 or 38 inch ram.

7. Judging the score of a big bull can be tricky, but the experts agree on a few points. A really big bull sports beams 55 inches or longer. When he throws his head back, his beam tips nearly touch the rump. The fourth point is nearly always the longest and its length should be 18 inches or greater. The brow point should be 14 inches or longer. To accumulate score fast, long fifth points help a lot and most high scoring elk have fifth points nearly as long as the fourth.

As Roosevelt elk live in thick timber one seldom gets a chance to look them over. Six pointers in themselves are rare, so I doubt if many mature bulls are ever passed up. This subspecies tends to have extra top points like the European red deer. This trait is called crowning and the trait indicates maturity.

8. What does it take to produce a big bull? Stated most simply — age. Gary Wolfe, formerly of Vermejo Park, a large private ranch managed for elk in New Mexico, and now a biologist for the Rocky Mountain Elk Foundation, has found the following at Vermejo Park. Six by six bulls are usually 4 1/2 or older. All bulls scoring 300 B&C points or greater were at least 4 1/2. Nearly 90 percent were 6 1/2 or older. Maximum antler development occurs between 7 1/2 and 10 1/2. Management policies in many states are not conducive for elk living to full maturity.

9. There seems to be a lot of confusion on the correct nomenclature of different size elk antlers. According to the B & C record book a six pointer is a royal, a seven an imperial and an eight a monarch.

10. Dale Burk, as successful as he is, does not always use a horse to reach the backcountry. He feels that his willingness to walk beyond other hunters gives him an advantage over nearly all other sportsmen in the field. He believes hard work is the key which puts the hunter into a remote location with little human pressure.

Atcheson says that as long as there is security cover for the elk, it may as likely be found near a road as way back in. Any location ignored by the bulk of hunters may prove to be an an elk's security pocket. Short valleys across a river may be totally unhunted. Use your imagination.

11. Hunting in areas with limited permits definitely gives the hunter an edge. It takes six years or so to grow a large bull elk, so anything that reduces the odds of a bull being killed, increases the trophy bull segment of the population. Atcheson has found that clients drawing tags in areas with light pressure generally have an easy time in making a kill.

12. Hunting on private property with limited availability to the sportsman can provide better odds of collecting a large bull. Hunter numbers must be low in comparison to elk numbers. Reduction of hunting pressure encourages an abundance of security zones. Many experts suggest that hunting bulls on intensively managed private properties can in no way be compared to elk hunting on public land, as they may not be nearly as wary. Hunting on the better properties can be very expensive.

13. An elk is a large animal, so some thought needs be given as to how he can be brought out. Traditionally he is hunted by horseback, but most hunters head to the hills on their own two feet. Dale Burk worries little where his bull drops, as he is fully prepared to carry him out on a packframe. Dale says he carries most of his animals as four full quarters. He has seldom boned the carcass of its meat. In contrast, Hilton says why wear yourself out toting extra weight, so he bones his elk. We always bone any large animal that has to be carried very far.

14. The importance of hunting first and last light varies from hunter to hunter and his own techniques. If you are to catch one feeding in the open, being afield during the first minutes of pre-dawn's light is essential. Dale Burk, who is essentially a stillhunter, says he does not worry about what time of day it is. Larry Hilton feels that a rutting bull is most active during the first part of the morning.

15. Hunting before a major storm and during cold weather definitely increase one's odds of scoring. Wildlife in general feed actively just before a storm. We have found that if air temperatures are pushing zero then game must eat more to survive. Last fall I spent two weeks hunting with chill factors ranging from 50-70 below. Big game was feeding at all hours.

A bull elk bugles during a snowstorm. Photo by Paul Johnson.

Noel Feather with Montana bull taken on a hunt guided by Larry Hilton. Photo by Larry Hilton.

16. When skies are clear and the moon is full, wildlife tend to feed at night, heading to security soon after morning's first rays of light.

17. Glassing for elk is not a common method of hunting, as they are a creature of the forest. In some high country areas a few bulls will gather their harems high above any forest. Here they are able to spot approaching enemies from afar. In this environment, binoculars are a handy tool. Field glasses and spotting scopes are also most useful tools for locating animals in many of the more open timber stands of the west. Try to avoid driving your quarry from his security zone — skirt the edges and glass into his home. I hunt bears in this same manner.

Atcheson suggests that a hunter in suitable country quickly glass for elk at first light. If nothing of interest is seen, then move to the next vantage point. Cover as much ground as possible until something of interest is seen. As a backup, the hunter should pick a secondary place to hunt if the first doesn't prove fruitful.

Jack notes that elk usually stand motionless for a period before bedding.

18. The choice of a weapon for elk is probably a dangerous issue and serious hunters will praise anything from 243's to 375 H&H's. Jack O'Conner swore by the 270 with 130 grain bullets. I have killed several myself with this combination, but I must confess I think it is a mite on the light side. Probably the 30 magnums are nearer to ideal, and maybe the 8 mag or the 338 might be number one choices. I killed one with a 375 in the lower chest, and had to trail it for two miles before getting in the final shot. I think it should be conceded if light calibers are used, like 6 mm's, 243's, and the 257 Roberts, there will probably be a lot of wounded elk left in the hills unless only ideal shots are taken.

Even though I think the 270 is a bit light, I still consider it my normal elk rifle. My good friend, Larry Hilton, has hunted elk all over the West, and has been in on 39 bull kills. He says that his 270 Winchester with 150 grain bullets is his elk rifle. Most of his personal kills have been with a bow. Jack Atcheson Sr., who has killed more big bulls than any human I know, totes a 338WM. He says a mature bull is a large animal and that the 7mm mag should be the minimum used.

Jack Atcheson feels that the elk hunter should always aim for the far shoulder, which ensures that the bullet will travel through the maximum number of inches of animal material.

19. Hunting during the rut without a doubt vastly increases a hunter's chances of killing a bull. As Larry Hilton puts it, hunting during the rut is like daytime, and pursuing bulls out of the rut is like the black of night. I feel that a good bow hunter during the rut has a much better chance of scoring than a rifle hunter out of the bugle season. I can prove this statement.

In stark comparison, Atcheson has little enthusiasm for hunting in the rut. He says so often conditions won't be right and the bulls don't bugle. He does note that hunters hearing bulls at least know there are some elk in the area.

20. The use of a bugle is what makes the rut such a dynamic time to collect a trophy. The full bugle of a bull elk is a series of notes of ever higher pitch. Not every hunter is able to duplicate this erie sound of the wilderness. Many successful hunters say that all one needs to do is duplicate the easy-to-imitate cow sounds. Squeals are easier to imitate than a full bugle and are also effective. There are many cassette tapes on the market to help the beginning caller. Many hunters feel that there are so many hunters learning to bugle that bulls are being forced to become less vocal.

21. What type call is best? Without question, in this age of sophisticated elk, the mouth diaphragm is best, with all others being second best. For many hunters diaphragms are difficult to master, but what in life that is worthwhile is easy. I have had trouble in learning to master the technique, but after a great many months of practice, I am near success.

22. What diaphragm calls are best? The hotshots in this part of Montana don't seem to agree on the best brand. Some prefer thin reeds, while others like the thicker ones. I started a few months ago, and I seem to have an easier time with a thin reeded diaphragm like those made by Cedar Hill Game Call Co.

As to grunt tubes, good callers seem to vary in their preferences. Larry Hilton swears by his 18-inch-long tube of inch and half ABS plastic. Gordon Michens, a very successful local elk hunter, uses inch and a half flex tubing.

23. It is one thing to get within rifle range of a bull with a call and quite another with a bow. Top archers give the following advice. Human scent needs to be reduced to a minimum. Knowledgeable hunters wash their clothes with baking soda to neutralize odors, and then induce masking scents by placing garments in a plastic bag with plant parts such as yarrow, pine bows, etc.

Many bowhunters are using cow elk urine to mask human odors. Gordon Michens says that he so successfully masks human odors that he doesn't even care which way the wind is blowing.

The final proof is success, and with a bow that means getting the bull to approach within 30 yards or less. It is relatively easy to get a bull to walk within rifle range, but those last few yards show who the real experts are. Knowing where to station oneself and still allow a clear shot is essential.

24. Tracking in the snow is a viable method of hunting bulls, but one that is understood by few sportsmen. Jack Atcheson Sr. says he has collected about two-thirds of his elk by tracking. It is a method by which the beginner will probably drive his quarry clear out of the territory. A bull once he is jumped from his security area will leave for parts unknown. You must be able to move in on your intended target and earn a shot before he is alarmed. Spook him from his feeding area and he will move to a nearby alternate, but scare him in his bedding grounds and he is gone.

25. Elk is considered to be near the top of the list as wild meats go. We have eaten meat from younger animals that we feel is as tasty and tender as prime corn-fed beef. I asked local Montana butcher Gordon Michens about meat yield from large elk. He says a fully mature, 800 to 900 pound, bull will yield about 475 pounds of bone-in meat or 330 pounds of boneless meat. This yield is assuming that there is no shot-up meat, and the skinned carcass is clean with little waste.

Chapter Sixteen

SHORT COURSE ON PRONGHORN HUNTING

When I moved to Montana in 1976, I had two pronghorns to my credit. Already they were one of my favorite big game animals. In order to ensure drawing my third tag, I applied in Montana and Wyoming, and received tags in both states. My goal was that I would learn how to hunt antelope by allocating two full weeks to the project. My neighbors thought me crazy. No one in Montana goes antelope hunting for more than a day, or maybe two at the most. During 1976 and 1977, I devoted a total of nearly 30 days to learning the art of pronghorn antelope hunting. Much of this time was spent with my good friend, Russ Moody. We crawled after dozens of bucks just to see how close we could get. Each fall one of the high points of the hunting season is the Gilchrist family antelope hunt. Besides myself, my three younger sons still at home love the sport. We are so efficient that on the ranch that we generally hunt, any animal we want might as well sign over his life to us.

We don't claim to be the best pronghorn hunters in the world, but we have sure learned a bunch of tricks that help increase our odds.

1. Try to pick broken country to hunt, so you have a fair chance of completing a stalk undetected. If the country is so rough, or brushy as to impede vision, the running pronghorn will avoid it.

2. In broken country antelope tend to follow definite movement patterns. Once learned by the hunter, he can use this information to good advantage year after year.

3. Antelope do not seem to be as alarmed about a horizontal object as they are a vertical one. Upright objects probably signify man and danger. A horizontal object probably is associated with a four-legged animal. I have cralwed to within 100 yards, or less, of many good bucks knowing they could see me.

4. As a stalking aid, sew leather patches on the knees and elbows on your antelope hunting clothes. Without this added protection the antelope hunter will invariably soon be filled with cacti spines.

5. As most antelope are shot at long range, I like to have a rest with me at all times. A pillow or day pack filled with styrafoam pellets is my usual rest.

6. As antelope are visible at such long range, some sort of rangefinder is desirable. The points of a 4X Leupold Duplex Reticle subtend exactly 16 inches at 100 yards, which is the width of the average antelope buck's body. Simple arithmetic shows that from the center of the crosshairs to the tip of a duplex post will subtend 16 inches at 200 yards, and half that distance 16 inches at 400 yards. Using a scope's duplex, you should be able to make shots that you formerly thought impossible. Of course the

The antelope buck the author shot at 588 yards. It should be noted that he used a styrafoam filled pillow as a rest.

Author's son, Brian, with his 1986 14-inch Montana buck.

hunter must know the trajectory of his rifle. I shoot a 270 with 130 grain Sierra boattails backed with 57.5 grains of H205. I am sighted in to be 3 inches high at 100. This puts me 4 inches high at 200, on at about 275, 10 inches low at 400 and 27 inches low at 500 yards. During the 1985 season I shot two antelope, and these were the only two fired at. The first was at a paced 412 yards and the second proved to be the longest known distance kill I have ever made — 588 yards. He also proved to be my best pronghorn trophy.

7. Judging horn length is not too difficult. When viewed from the front, if the horns appear to stand twice as high as the ears are long, then you are looking at a 12 1/2 or 13 inch antelope, which is not a good head. To have a decent trophy, the horns need to stand two and a half times the ear height, and will be in the 14 inch class. Three ear lengths and the hunter looking at a top head, of over 15 inches. Anything over 15 is a trophy of a lifetime that should score high in the record books.

8. We rough butcher our game in the field, keeping the front shoulders and hams intact while boning the remainder of the carcass. Last fall the boys and I weighed the meat from several antelope bucks and found the average yield to be 60 pounds. By comparison, we found the average doe yields 50 pounds.

Stuart Gilchrist with a buck he shot at 125 yards by waiting on top of a butte while the author kept driving about in a large fenced-in pasture. He had his pick of several animals and decided on this heavy 14 1/2 animal that scored over 78 B&C points.

9. In looking at a herd, bucks are generally to the front, or the rear when running. In large groups, you will also sometimes find a buck or two in the center.

10. Ambushing antelope is fast becoming my favorite method of hunting this cunning creature of the plains. They seem to travel the same routes over and over. By staying concealed at the top of a butte, near a water hole, or close to a high spot in a barbed wire fence, the hunter is almost certain to find shooting.

11. As I delve deeper into the sport of antelope hunting, it has been found that pushing them to a prelocated hunter is quite easy. Antelope seem to like to follow fences and drainage patterns. Stationing hunters in selected spots has allowed us to get shots at individual animals that are almost unstalkable. After posting one, or more, of my sons, or a client, in my selected spot, I gradually move the herd. We have pushed pronghorns three miles to exactly where wanted.

12. Never shoot into the herd. During the fall of 1977, my good friend from Juneau, Alaska, Al Kadush, spent nearly two months hunting and fishing with me in Montana. We had stalked to within 150 yards of a large band of pronghorns containing a good herd buck. Even though the buck was surrounded by does, Al tried a shot rather than wait until the buck was in the clear. My friend ended up hanging his tag on a doe. It is so easy to have an unwanted animal walk into the path of your bullet. HOLD YOUR FIRE UNLESS YOUR INTENDED TARGET IS IN THE CLEAR! On several occasions I have seen two animals killed with one shot.

13. Never shoot into a running band if you want trophy heads. Many a hunter has shot into a running herd of animals only to hit the wrong one. At two hundred yards it is easy to hit an animal two or three behind the one you are trying to collect.

14. We bone our antelope in the field. My family loves antelope meat. In contrast, many hunters claim that the meat has a strong objectionable taste. Maybe our instant skinning accounts for the fact that our meat taste so good. Even people that don't normally like pronghorn meat say it is wonderful when Pat prepares it. We remove the hams and front shoulders and bone the balance. By placing the meat into three game bags it cools quickly, which maybe accounts for the good flavor.

15. The author's wife, Pat, thinks that antelope meat is the best stew meat there is because of its unique flavor.

Montana antelope buck. Photo by Larry Hilton.

16. Finding crossing points along fence lines will virtually ensure success. Antelope seldom jump fences, so if they want to change pastures they must crawl under. If the pasture is enclosed with a sheep-tight fence, a pronghorn will spend his entire life in this single fenced in area. If hunting pressure is light, antelope don't seem to want to crawl under barbed wire. With pressure they will readily go under the wire. I have noticed that they usually crawl through fences at the same point, time and time again. Crossing points are usually found near fence corners. If you can find an ambush spot near a crossing, leave someone in hiding while the hunting vehicle goes about its business. If you are organized, I believe the man sitting will probably have a better chance of scoring on a good head than the hunter in the vehicle.

17. A spotting scope is almost essential for judging trophy pronghorns. Binoculars just won't allow you tell the difference between a 13, 14 or a 15 at long range. Antelope are so spooky of humans the hunter is best advised to glass from the vehicle. Several firms sell window mounts which permit easy scoping from a hunting car, without opening the door.

18. Don't get out of your vehicle to glass a herd in the distance. Stay inside. Antelope will often run, even though you are a mile away, when you step from your vehicle.

19. Walk over hills. When one is driving a vehicle over a rise where you can't see what is on the other side, stop short of the crest and walk. We have managed to surprise many a buck using this tactic.

20. Pronghorns seem to run over two ridges when alarmed in hilly country. If the terrain is broken and once spooked, a herd will seldom be found over the first rise, but very often over the next. This trait has been consistent enough that it has yielded us many shots.

21. Gumbo is the bane of antelope hunters, and is what the locals call the high clay content soil when it is wet. After a rain, the ground turns to gumbo and will defy movement by any vehicle including 4WD's. A man on foot will soon stand inches higher. There is no real way to beat gumbo.

22. Although most states in the West have pronghorns, Wyoming and Montana are of the most interest to hunters. Trophies can be found most anywhere, but notable areas are the Red Desert of Wyoming (Units 56, 57,58) and the units around Jordan, Montana. Some of the largest heads are being taken in Arizona, but permits are very limited. Odds for securing a permit by the nonresident are excellent in both Wyoming and Montana, and cost approximately $100 in either state.

Chapter Seventeen

SHORT COURSE ON CARIBOU HUNTING

Of all the big game species, I have collected more caribou than any other. During the 60's the legal limit over much of Alaska was four, with the season opening August 1 and running to March 31 — a period of eight months. Although I have taken many caribou, my experience has been limited to the state of Alaska. In the 49th state I have hunted the species in a variety of habitats, ranging from the muskegs of the Gulkana Basin to the high mountain peaks of the Wrangells and the Alaska Range, and on to the rivers of the North Slope of the Brooks Range. Of all antlered species, he has the potential to grow more pounds of antler per hundred weight of body size than any other. And yet, he has never reached the status on the trophy room wall that he deserves. Why? He is too common, much like the beautiful impala of Africa.

1. The most definite statement that can be made about caribou is that they are unpredictable to the point of extremes. I have seen them spook from a well-executed stalk at 500 yards, run over the hill for five miles, stop to wonder what they were fleeing from, and then quickly return, stopping to stare from 50 yards. Because of this trait, never despair for lack of stalking cover. They might let you walk up to them even though they know you are there.

2. I have never felt that it took a lot of firepower to down this animal of the North. I have shot them with a wide array of calibers from a 225 to the 375 H&H. The most were killed with a 257 Roberts and several with handguns. I can't remember ever having a problem in killing one.

Author with his first trophy caribou shot in the Gulkana basin of southcentral Alaska. This magnificent bull has excellent mass on top, double shovels, but poor bez points. B&C score 391 1/8.

3. If you are trying to collect a large bull the best way to achieve success is to hunt during the migration. If you happen to be at a point where large numbers are funneling through, you may see thousands per day. If you are selective, and can judge them, sooner or later you should score on that record book head.

4. The double shovel caribou has been mentioned by many outdoor writers as if he were among the rarer trophies of the world. Some authors state that a mountable double shovel might be as rare as 1 in 10,000. I have taken at least three good double shovels and have guided hunters to several others. I have only guided a few caribou hunters. Some people would have you believe that a double shovel will magically add points to the B&C score. Not so. Often the mass of two shovels will only equal the size of one outstanding shovel. From looking at the B&C record book, I would guess that 25 percent of all listed caribou have double shovels.

5. Many persons, including guides, have told me that they consider judging a trophy caribou to be quite difficult. I have never felt that a good to outstanding head was that hard to discern. His antlers are composed of six main elements: the shovel(s), the bez points, length of main beam, the rear points, the top and the inside spread. The rear points seldom amount to much, being only a few inches long, so they can be pretty much ignored when judging the animal. Most mature bulls have antlers approaching 50 inches or more (not true with woodland caribou and sometimes mountain caribou), so antler length has not been a major criteria in my trophy judging. Look for a well developed shovel or shovels, good bez points and a top that is either palmated or has two long points.

The three B&C measurements that I mentally study, when I am judging a caribou are:

F-4 Length of second longest top point

F-5 Length of longest top point

H-4 Circumference at smallest place between the two longest top palm points

These three measurements are interrelated and are the key to a high score. Both sides must have two long points on top with the narrowest point between them being wide and hopefully the two sides matching. After deductions, in essence, it is the smaller of two antlers that counts for the final score. Only the two longest points on top count for length. If the third longest point was 18 inches instead of six inches, it would only be counted as a point and add 1 0/8 to the score. The two sides must match, or the score will not add up fast. Commonly, one of the major elements will be missing which keeps the head from being a top trophy. I have seen many a head that has length, a super shovel and bezes but only had short points on top like John Colclough's trophy in the photo shown. On other occasions the head has it all except a good bez; such was the case with my Gulkana Basin bull.

6. Most antlered big game species have a normal antler configuration, such as the typical 4 by 4 muley , or   whitetails always   have all points growing from the main beam, or the 6 by 6 is the typical mature elk, with the 4th point nearly always being the longest. Not so with the bull caribou except he will have a shovel or shovels, a bez, a rear point and a cluster of something on top. Some bulls have single points growing from the top of the main beam. Others have points growing from a palmated top while some will exhibit a dominate point sprouting from the main beam with secondary points growing from the dominant point. Commonly, caribou bulls grow mismatched antlers. Finding animals whose right and left sides look alike can be difficult. Sometimes one sees hundreds of mature bulls in a day and yet finds nothing that is wanted.

7. Many trophy hunters collect their bull caribou while on a sheep hunt, long before the velvet has been stripped. It is almost impossible to retain the velvet, without damage, as moisture allows it to rot away. In addition, mechanical action will grind away enough to give a moth-eaten appearance. The velvet needs to be stripped, which can be readily done with a pocket knife to pull the furry substance off. If the antlers have not hardened, the tips of many points may rot away. A taxidermist can build them out again, but they will not be real and of course cannot be counted in the B&C score. In northern Alaska, I have found that antlers are hard by August 17th. If a bull in that part of the world is shot after that date the point tips will not rot away. What the date is in other areas I cannot say, but it should be similar.

Author with a huge Alaska Range bull that he and John Colclough collected many years ago. The main beams on this animal were an impressive 59 7/8 inches. B&C score 374 7/8.

8. Bleaching stripped antlers is desirable if they are to be stained later. We have thrown antlers into a creek for several days with flowing water removing the blood from the semi-hardened antlers. Once completed, they seem to stain more readily than untreated antlers.

9. Both sexes have antlers, but cows never grow a set large enough to even approach minimal trophy size.

The high scoring Brooks Range caribou boast double shovels plus it is the only bull the author has ever seen with double rear points. B&C score 374-plus.

10. There are many subspecies of caribou and their ranges often cross. The old-timers around the Chistochina area of Alaska used to claim that both the barren ground caribou and the much larger woodland caribou lived locally. I used to laugh. On a trip to the head of this drainage, John Colclough took a huge bull with 59 7/8 inch main beams. This animal was nearly the size of a spike bull elk. A few days later only two miles away, I shot what looked to be a huge bull. He and the rest of the herd proved to be miniatures compared to John's trophy. His antlers only taped 43 inches and his body was probably comparable to a so-so whitetail.

11. If he were not so common, plus being easy to hunt at certain times, the species would rank with America's top trophies. No other animal grows headgear so large in proportion to his size as the bull caribou. With his long, silky white neck he is an animal of beauty that is seldom equalled anywhere.

12. It should be noted that as the rut progresses the bull's neck begins to develop a dewlap or bell like appendage. If it is not opened when skinning it will spoil, allowing the hair to slip.

The author shot this smallish Alaska Range double shovel bull many years ago along the Chistochina River. Because of the unusual antler conformation, the author saved the antlers, which he still owns.

13. As the rut approaches, the bull's cape changes color by acquiring a beautiful white neck. If the hunter wants a quality cape he should wait as long as possible during his sojourn, before collecting his caribou. Early in the season the neck will be an uninteresting gray.

14. In some areas bulls migrate ahead of cows. This appears to be true in both the Arctic and Porcupine herds of Alaska. Hemming, in ADF&G's "The Distribution Movement Patterns Of Caribou In Alaska," notes that during the fall migration on the Alaska Peninsula that the bulls follow the cows. He further states that with some of the minor herds, all seasonal movement is either up or down. When the Nelchina herd was at its peak during the 60's, I never noted any large groups of bulls. It is a real thrill to be surrounded by a herd of 100 percent mature bulls, sometimes numbering in the hundreds. I have no idea of the herd movements in Quebec.

15. Caribou dislike heat. During the hot days of summer and early fall, they can be found lying on alpine snow patches, or glaciers and on the lowland icefields one sees along the northern rivers. They predictably rest on ice to such a degree that I have often concentrated my hunting efforts around ice. Even in the winter caribou like ice, as they often bed in the middle of a lake. Back in the days when one could fly and hunt the same day, many caribou were shot standing beside one's plane just after you'd landed on a lake.

16. When planning a stalk on caribou it is normally futile to attempt to follow them, as their usual walking and feeding speed is too rapid. One should try to intercept the herd.

17. Crawling may be the most effective method to stalk a caribou when you are caught in the open. Game seems to associate man as being vertical, while a horizontal object is most often assumed to be another animal. A man on horseback can often approach a lot closer than can the human afoot. I have pulled off this latter ploy most effectively.

18. As is true with all animals that congregate, don't shoot into the herd. You may kill a caribou that you don't want, or maybe you will shoot more than one. Twice I have fired three shots at a herd and killed four. At the time this was acceptable as the yearly limit was four, and I was meat hunting anyway. Think of the consequences if you were head hunting, or if the limit was one.

19. This animal of the North can cover ground faster than any species that I know of. Commonly, he will travel 30 or 40 miles a day. If there is much herd movement it is best to position one's self in a funnel type location and wait. One should constantly be seeing new animals if it is migration time.

20. The use of binoculars and/or spotting scope is almost essential in hunting trophy caribou, as it is with all open country animals. A 20X scope can save many a wasted mile walked to check an animal that wasn't quite large enough. I have seen times that it was even difficult to tell the difference between waving willow bushes and caribou antlers at two miles.

21. Caribou can be found as high as sheep and often are. Many a good bull has been taken by a sheep hunter. Some of the difficult alpine terrain that caribou can negotiate is amazing. I have seen many good trophy bulls while on Dall sheep hunts. Wherever one can find caribou lichen, one can find the species.

22. The species is commonly hunted during the rut when it is most unwary, and might even be considered as dumb. No wonder it has a reputation for being easy to hunt. Before the rut, hunting caribou can be totally frustrating. He deserves more credit than he usually gets.

23. The caribou's reputation as a source of meat is generally downgraded. Many say the meat is hardly edible. Most claim the meat must be well cooked, to be safe, as the species is supposed to be infected with all sorts of parasites. It is claimed that the meat is very low in protein value and

Author's wife, Pat, with her late season Chistochina River cow caribou.

that a man can starve to death eating it. Actually, can a human subsist 100 percent on any kind of meat?

We have always found the meat to be quite dry, so Pat always covered roasts with foil and cooked it under a very low heat of about 300 F. This method allows her to retain as much moisture as possible. We like to slice steaks extremely thin, which allows for almost instant cooking, thereby preserving moisture. Sue Arthur cooked caribou steaks for me several times on the rare side, and they were fantastic. She feels the danger from parasites is minimal.

24. Although one sometimes sees caribou by the thousands, their density is low when one considers the total area of their range. The hunter merely enjoys the illusion of high density, as he is pursuing the animal when it is concentrated during the migration. The species may also be concentrated during calving. I had the opportunity to observe and photograph from the air, the Nelchina herd on their calving range, at the head of the Talkeetna River. ADF&G estimated, that spring, that there were 40,000 cows on 30 square miles.

The primary food of the caribou is reindeer lichen (Cladonia alpestris), which will produce on prime range four tons per acre in 50 years. In the Lower 48, good grassland will easily yield four tons per acre per year. It is physically impossible to have a high overall density of caribou.

Chapter Eighteen

LAND OF THE GIANT RAMS

My fellow hunters are constantly saying to me, "If only I had been born a generation ago I could have really killed some super trophies." Ten years ago I might have agreed with that statement, but not in 1986. Today, game departments are managing for quality as well as quantity. Biological knowledge of how to enhance wildlife is becoming fine-tuned.

Jack O'Connor hunted North America's game fields as they were being opened in the Far North. He should have seen hunting at its best. Did he? His works continually state that the taking of a 40-inch ram is an almost impossible goal. Chadwick may of killed the largest officially recorded ram in North America, but his diary tells of a general scarcity of game. They rode long distances just to find any big game. The country had been depleted by unregulated meat hunting, with wolves hammering at what was left.

Leland Crow, who is Grand Slammer Number Six and now 84 years old, hunted northern Canada and Alaska "back when." Is his home filled with mighty rams? Yes, but not with ones he shot. Leland has killed nine sheep himself and has yet to claim a large specimen. Leland has been there and he is still a hunter of the first order.

Some species seem to be adding few new entries to the record book, like Alaskan brown bear. It takes too long to grow a true trophy brownie. Most will be shot long before they reach ripe old age, but there are still some old boars around. The same is generally true of elk. It takes 7 1/2 years to grow a large set of elk antlers, and over most of his range he has little chance of living this long.

The 80's mark some bright spots for the trophy hunter, especially the

Montana bighorn ram.

sheep hunter. Look at any issue of *Wild Sheep*, the quarterly publication of the Foundation for North American Wild Sheep (FNAWS). Its pages are filled with photos of giant wild rams, many of which break the magical 40 inch mark. Game departments throughout the sheep's range seem to be recognizing the importance of quality horns. Sheep populations of southern Canada and the U.S. seem to have reached a low point and are now rebounding. Transplants are filling available ranges. Sheep hunting is available on a drawing basis throughout the West in every state with a viable population except California, which maybe open soon.

I believe that I live in the best state for the big game hunter in the United States south of the Canadian border. Montana is where the game is, which seems to be no secret. Our 17,000 nonresident general licenses sold out the day they went on sale in 1987.

After living in the Bitterroot Valley a short time, I began hearing from some of the more serious local hunters about the phenomenal horn growth of the East Fork herd (Unit 270). This was a new herd that had been introduced from the Sun River in 1972. Local enthusiasts were trying to photograph the bigger rams and Hamilton taxidermist Phil Healey soon enticed me into looking for rams with my Super Cub. It didn't seem at the time like anyone knew where the rams summered. Eventually, I found them. Phil called one day that fall, and asked me to age a ram that a hunter had just brought in from 270. Try as I could, the 3/4 plus curl ram could only be aged as 2 1/2 years. This was a far cry from the usual 4 1/2 years it takes a Dall to reach the same size. To top it off, that young bighorn boasted 15-inch bases. I was impressed. F&G records show that one unit 270 ram reached 40 3/8 inches, around the curl, in just 4 1/2 years. During the 1978 season a local hunter, Sandy Rose, killed a ram in the same unit that later scored 188 4/8.

The neighboring West Fork of the Bitterroot (Unit 250) also has a sheep population, but is a native herd. Biologists state that this population has the most complex migration route of any bighorn herd in North America. Instead of fast-growing horns, these sheep do not produce good heads. By studying eight years of records, I learned that the largest ram harvested only had a 35 5/8 inch horn length.

Stories of giant rams began to circulate about the Thompson Falls country of westernmost Montana. Rumor had it that rams harvested from one unit were large, either scoring close to the "Book", or having at least one horn measuring 40 inches. Most hunters in the know started applying for permits in the Thompson Falls area. Finally, in 1979 Armand Johnson established a new Montana state record by killing a Thompson Falls ram with a score of 200 3/8 B&C when officially measured after the 60 day drying period. Three years later when remeasured by a panel the score dropped to 197 1/8. The long horn measured an incredible 45 4/8 inches.

The Unit 121 herd was established in 1959 with Sun River stock. This is one of the larger herds in the state, numbering almost 500 animals. The 1984 edition of *Montana Big Game Trophies* lists 9 of 58 sheep with a score of 180, or more, coming from Sanders County, (Units 121 and 123).

During the winter of 1977 and 1978, Montana sheep enthusiasts were appalled that the Wildhorse Island herd had grown so large that a major die-off occurred. It was estimated that 40 sheep perished, many of them mature rams. The state was able to salvage a few horns but many were taken before Fish and Game officials entered on the scene. In June of 1978, the state held a auction to sell those Wildhorse Island horns. The two largest sets had unofficial scores of 190 2/8 and 188 3/8. Many of the horns that were privately salvaged easily made 180 B&C points. Imagine, all these top trophies came from one small island of a few hundred acres.

News was made again in 1982 when Bonnie Ford collected an outsized ram in newly opened Unit 203, near Petty/Graves Creeks, west of Missoula. Her ram was scored by B&C officials at 197 0/8 with the longest horn taping 44 0/8 inches. Once again, an introduced herd from the Sun River was involved.

For the past decade Montana, has been producing one or more record book rams a season. Then, in 1980 six were recorded. Suddenly, in 1984, a whopping 10 recorded with an estimated six from the newly-opened upper Rock Creek herd (Unit 216). Three have been officially scored and entered into the state record book. Rock Creek rancher and guide Larry Clark told me that this herd had nearly died out and the rams were runts with horns seldom exceeding 33 or 34 inches. In 1975, 31 sheep were planted in the area from the Sun River. Was the introduction a success? You bet! The season was reopened in 1983 with eight permits. Six of the eight sheep were reported to score 180 B&C points or greater. Two have been officially scored to qualify for the state record book.

In 1984, a huge ram was taken by Larry Smith, who was guided by Tim Magness of Anaconda. This sheep officially scored 199 points, with the longest horn being 43 2/8 inches, and boasting 16 inch bases. The same season Steven Gingras killed a Rock Creek ram with a score of 195 1/8. His trophy has an outstanding 16 6/8 inch base. Bob Watts, a Montana hunter, scored on another ram with 17 1/4 bases. Wow! Aerial counts taken during the spring of 1984 show there are almost 200 sheep in this herd.

Last winter I gave a hunting seminar at nearby Anaconda. Local sheep nuts claim there is still a ram in the area that may be larger than Smith's trophy.

A short distance from the Rock Creek herd can be found the South Flint Range herd, which lies near the old mining city of Anaconda. This population was established in 1967, again from Sun River stock. The original 26 sheep increased to an inventoried 154 by 1984. In 1983, the first season was opened with five permits. In the November 1983 *Wild Sheep* magazine, Keith Atcheson reported that unit 213 yielded a 6 1/2 year old ram with a 45-inch horn and a 17 3/4 base. Compare this to sheep coming from many areas where it takes about 10 years to grow an outstanding trophy. On a recent field trip to Unit 213, the author saw a single band with 51 rams.

In 1985, the quota was increased to 10 with the result that six book rams were harvested, including one by Bob Bede of my town of Hamilton. His ram scores 187 3/8 with an impressive long horn of 45 4/8 (official). Only seven sheep in the 1981 Boone and Crockett record book have a horn measurement that will equal, or exceed, Bede's trophy. Bob told me that he only spent four days, including scouting trips, after rams. After he dropped his mighty sheep, 10 more rams appeared from the trees and stood staring. He feels that the largest would equal the one he killed.

Montana biologist Shawn Stewart gave me these figures on the 1985 Unit 213 harvest: Of 10 rams, five exceeded the magical length of forty: 46 2/8 (green), 44 4/8, 42 3/8, 40 3/8 and 40 4/8. Neighboring Unit 216 yielded three 40-inch rams with the longest taping 42 3/8. I think the good old days must be the 1980's!

Another view of Bede's Unit 213 ram. He saw 18 rams the day he scored. When the ram was first shot, the left horn measured an impressive 46 1/4 inches. Photo courtesy Bob Bede.

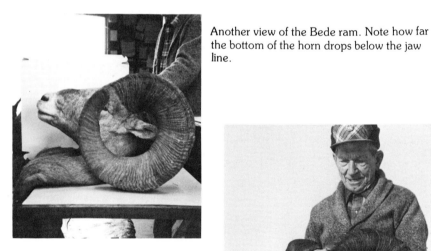

Another view of the Bede ram. Note how far the bottom of the horn drops below the jaw line.

Photo courtesy Big Sky Taxidermy Hamilton, Montana.

Leland Crow with the Bob Bede's magnificent bighorn head. The left horn officially measures 45 4/8 inches. Only seven rams in the 1981 edition of the B&C record book will equal or exceed this length. It was taken in western Montana during the 1985 season. Six of ten rams shot in this unit in 1985 made the record book.

From
"Montana Big Game Trophies, 3rd Edition, 1984
And From F & G Records

Number of Bighorns with Score of 180 or Greater
Harvested Past Decade

Year	Number	
1985	14	
1984	10	(7 entered)
1983	?	(4 entered)
1982	3	
1981	1	
1980	6	
1979	2	
1978	7	
1977	1	
1976	1	

Some Montana bighorn sheep horns received at Big Sky Taxidermy – Hamilton, Montana during the 1985 season.

Position Lt to Rt	Unit Taken	Age Yrs.	Length Ins.	Base Ins.	B&C Score
1	270	4.5	35 7/8	14 4/8	———
2	270	4.5	35 2/8	16	176 4/8
3	213	9.5	46 4/8	14 7/8	187 3/8
4	270	5.5	36 2/8	16 1/8	178 2/8
5	270	4.5	Unknown	16 6/8	182+

These four rams from unit 270 represent all but one that was killed in this unit in 1985. Note that ram No. 5 was only 4.5 years old and yet will unofficially qualify for the record book. Where else but Montana? What would he have scored if he had lived to be 10?

Some Montana bighorn sheep horns received at Big Sky Taxidermy-Hamilton, Montana during the 1985 season.

The February 1986 issue of *Wild Sheep* quotes Montana sheep fanatic Jim Ford as saying 11 or 12 rams made the book from Montana in 1985. I know of at least one more. Imagine at least a dozen book heads in a single season?

What do sheep hunters think of Montana? The first "Governor's Permit" for a Montana bighorn was auctioned at the 1986 FNAWS convention in Hawaii. It brought the all-time high for an auctioned sheep permit at $79,000. The previous top figure was $67,500 for a Nevada desert sheep permit in 1983.

A man in good condition should be able to score on a top record book ram, as the tag is good anywhere it is legal to hunt sheep in Montana. A hunter could start in the East Fork (270) on Monday morning, drive for a couple of hours to Rock Creek (216), hunt the afternoon, then drive for another hour to unit 213.

The buyer, filmmaker Art Dubs, spent considerable time looking over rams before harvesting a high-scoring head from the Petty Creek area near Missoula. Dubs also purchased the States's second permit at the FNAWS 1987 convention at Nashville for the generous sum of $109,000. He must have liked what he saw in Montana during the 1986 season.

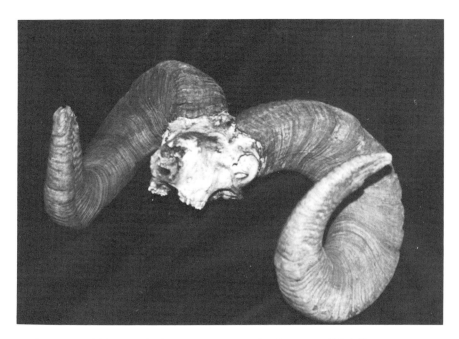

Another outsized Montana bighorn ram that unofficially scores 183 4/8.

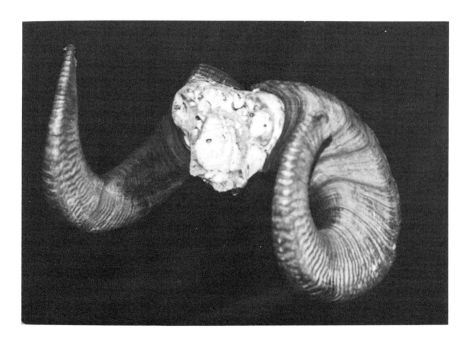

This Montana ram scores 177 4/8. The right horn tapes 38 inches.

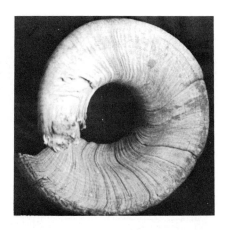

Two views of a single Montana sheep horn. This single tapes 40 3/4 inches long with a 15 1/4 inch base and scores 95 0/8. If this was a complete set it would have no trouble in making high record book.

The serious sheep hunter should begin to wonder why there are so many large rams even in these modern times? I did, and all fingers seemed to point at Shawn Stewart as the best source of information. Shawn has been compiling the state's bighorn harvest data for several years. When asked why Montana is producing so many large rams, he explained it this way: Most of the "Book" rams are coming from introduced herds that are from genetically desirable Sun River stock. The 1984 state record book shows 17 of 58 B&C rams coming from the Sun River. Most were taken many years ago but the genes must be there. Biologist Valerius Geist theorized in his book *Mountain Sheep* that quaility sheep were most likely to occur on new ranges with a low population density. Certainly the introduced bighorn herds of Montana meet these criteria.

When asked why big heads seem to occur in bunches, he said that the reason is that during a very mild winter when the rams were still lambs the survival rate would be abnormally high. There is a bonus of excellent initial horn growth. If this first season is followed by several years with mild winters, and good summer grass, this group of rams has a jump on sheep born in other years. There would also be more of them. Stewart hopes to correlate the data he has collected to prove that if the first three or four years of a ram's life are blessed with prime conditions, a super ram will be produced. Stewart warned that hunters seeing this high survival rate are apt to pressure the game commission into increasing the ram quota. This does not hurt the population, but it does decrease the odds of a ram living to old age. He feels, as do most students of trophy sheep, that it takes at least seven years to grow a true trophy. Any less time and there won't be the mass of an old rams horns. I got the feeling that Shawn does not think that management policies in Montana are conducive to truly big rams. He

Author accompanied Russ Moody on his 1986 Unit 270 sheep hunt. This 4 1/2-year-old ram measures 37 6/8 inches with 16 2/8 inch bases.

was very positive, however, in his thinking that Montana may soon produce more 200-point rams.

Our state should continue to grow "Book" rams for a while, for we have had many mild winters in a row.

Now that we have established that the state of Montana is the bighorn ram hunter's paradise, what are his chances of drawing a permit? In 1986, 8,555 persons applied for 610 sheep permits. If that sounds slim the odds aren't really that good, as many of these tags were for ewes or half curl rams. State regulations used to say that a maximum of 10 percent of the tags could go to nonresidents. If 10 tags were not available in a unit then a nonresident could not apply. Recently, the system has been changed, so nonresidents can more likely draw 10 percent of the permits. Areas open to the out-of-stater are changed each year, and in 1985 20 units were open to application. Upon checking the 1986 computer sheets, I found that three nonresidents drew ram tags, plus three more received ewe permits. In addition, 60 more held tags in the unlimited permit areas.

Will Montana produce the new world's record bighorn? Biologist Shawn Stewart seems to think that Montana will at least soon add another 200-point ram to the record book. An examination of the 1981 edition of the record book shows that there are 10 bighorn rams listed with a score of 200 or greater. All came from Canada. Most were harvested many years ago with the latest entry being 1955. Recently, a British Columbia game biologist gave me photos of two super rams. One boasts a 49 3/4 inch long horn. This sheep died a few years ago not too far from the Montana border. The second is reported to have burned, but was taped at 51 1/2 inches and may have scored as much as 214 B & C points. The world record was killed in 1911 and scores 208 1/8. If management policies allow a ram to reach old age, Montana has a good chance of producing a new number one.

Chapter Nineteen

A GRAND SLAM OF BUCKS

Thoughts of far-off lands, majestic mountains and exotic animals run through the minds of most big game hunters. Even if your experiences go no further than your home state, it costs nothing to dream. What an enjoyable evening to be cast into a vicarious experience through the talents of a writer's pen — to far off Africa, or maybe to the Cassiar Mountains of central British Columbia. What could possibly surpass the mystic of Kodiak Island?

The late Jack O'Connor firmly implanted the thrill of hunting the wild ram upon the American public. He even messed up some people for life, like my good friend Leland Crow, who holds "Grand Slam of North American Wild Sheep" card number six. Crow reached his goal, spurred on by O'Connors writings, in 1959 by taking the four North American sheep species — Dall, stone, bighorn and desert. Today, hundreds have reached this coveted goal of collecting all North American sheep. Others have even gone beyond and are now collecting the "Super Slam," which consists of killing 12 of the world's 17 sheep species. Sounds expensive doesn't it? It is too. Today, if you shot the four North American species the first time around in a minimum of four hunts you would have spent an estimated $30,000. The cost of a Super Slam is so high only a very few even think about the project.

Dedicated sheep hunters have even formed an organization called the Foundation For North American Wild Sheep. This group has been accomplishing some major feats of wildlife management and habitat improvement throughout the West, Canada and Alaska. I would urge that all serious alpine hunters join this organization.

No doubt about it, sheep hunting is inspiring. Traveling over remote mountain ridges with some of the world's grandest scenery unfolding before you does leave a lasting impression on one's soul. Today, there are more persons wanting to pursue rams than there are opportunities, so the price has risen. The simple law of supply and demand is in control. There are others who experience the joys of high country hunting without mortgaging the family homestead. Deer in the alpine can provide the same joys without breaking the bank. One can collect the five species of North American deer recognized by the Boone and Crockett Club at a fraction of the cost of a taking a "slam" of rams. This record keeping organization list the recognized species as: whitetail, Coues', mule, Sitka blacktail and Columbian blacktail.

A collection of sheep on the wall is impressive, but is it any grander than a group of mighty deer heads? I don't think so. I have enjoyed roaming many of the game fields of the West and Alaska after having resided for a a decade and a half in our most northern state and 11 years in Montana. Having collected nearly 30 rams and mountain goats, what do I prefer to chase in Montana? The mule deer. He is plumb fun to pursue. He lives in a wide variety of habitats in the state that I have chosen as my home. In Montana, the muley is found in the rough mountaintops of the western third of the state, in the deep-timbered erosion courses of the Missouri Breaks, and the rolling plains of the eastern half of the state. As well as having collected several good mature muley bucks, I have scored on a mountable whitetail buck and several outstanding Sitka blacktails. I love to hunt them all.

The lure of giant antlers aroused my hunter's senses into seeking new experiences. Right now, I have plans for hunting the remaining two recognized deer species with my friend Ed Shoemaker, an exotic bird rancher and gunstock maker from southern California. Ed has been tremendously successful at the game of deer hunting. In fact, he is so dedicated to deer hunting that he collected a "Grand Slam" of the five North American deer species in just three years. As a bonus, he has an enviable track record in finding the burro deer of southern California, which is a hard-to-hunt subspecies of mule deer.

Ed is a man who has roamed the world's game fields like most of us only dream about. As a former owner of a large Zimbabwe farm, he has enjoyed the opportunity of chasing big game in Africa like few Americans. What does Ed Shoemaker have to say about deer hunting? On a recent visit to Montana he summed it up this way: "In my opinion, hunting dangerous game is the ultimate, with chasing deer a close second. After having shot a vast amount of plains animals in Africa, I found that deer hunting is much more satisfying than pursuing the African antelope species. I think I prefer Coues' deer. Don't know why. Maybe because I love the high desert habitat so much."

After having spent some five weeks in the field with Ed during the past two years, I have found that he has much to be proud of. His deer hunting accomplishments have all been reached without the help of a guide. He has much advice to offer both the new and the accomplished sportsman.

Ed began his deer hunting career years ago with the desert strain of the southern California mule deer, which is called the burro deer. This subspecies does not have the majestic antlers of the mighty mountain mule deer, or even the smaller antlers of the normal desert race. His 14 bucks and two does (on extra tags) in 14 consecutive years would be an impressive record anywhere, but in San Diego County it is doubly noteworthy as success in the area averages around 5 percent. After seeing the local habitat of dense 12-foot-tall brush, I knew why so few hunters score. I asked Ed what should be considered a good burro buck? He surprised me with his answer. "Any buck should be considered a trophy. They are that hard to find."

On a recent trip to his home, I had a firsthand opportunity to inspect my friend's trophies. His burro deer trophy sported antlers showing the typical 5 by 5 mule deer conformation, only in miniature, with an unimpressive 17-inch outside spread. This is the largest set of burro deer antlers he has ever seen in the field.

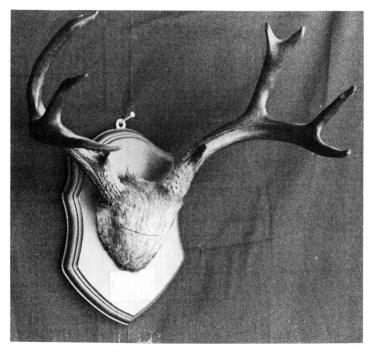

Ed's best burro deer was taken in 1966 near San Diego, California. It is the largest of the subspecies he has ever laid eyes on in a lifetime of successful deer hunting.

How does a man beat the odds of 5 percent success for 14 consecutive years? Ed was most willing to share his secrets. He started: "At least 10 of these bucks I collected by following a track after a rain. I look for a large track and stay on it until I either reach the end with the buck standing in the tracks, reach a no trespassing sign, or occasionally lose the trail. Tracking on bare soil that is not cluttered with moss and needles is not as hard as one would think, but it does take practice. It makes anyone a better hunter. After a rain it is easy to tell fresh sign from old." He continued, "Another very effective way to hunt is to wait at a water hole. Sooner or later you should see game, provided you are using the wind correctly. Another point to keep in mind is to find a productive pocket. Deer are not evenly distributed over their range. I hunt a pocket of another type. It is a pocket of public land that is totally surrounded by unhunted, posted private land. No one else seems to know about this pocket."

Because my friend enjoys a quality experience, he prefers low hunter densities. In southern California, he has found that the steep eastern slopes of the mountains, where they drop into the desert, are almost devoid of humans.

Ed actually started assembling his grand slam of trophy deer in 1983. During that single fall he collected his best Coues', his best Columbian blacktail, and his only whitetail.

As is typical of Coues' deer hunters, he did not score for the first three seasons. It seemed as if the animal was a rare and endangered species, though that is not the case. He kept at it and today the man feels that he can find plenty of bucks wherever the animal lives. For the past six seasons, one or more of these midget whitetails has fallen to his rifle. His prize of 1983 boast a 4 by 4 rack, a 14-inch outside spread, and a 104 B&C score. I asked my buddy what my chances would be of scoring on a buck next fall. He feels that using his methods a hunter should able to collect a mountable buck in five days.

Ed began his dissertation on pursuing the tiny desert whitetail: "The country where the Coues' lives looks like there should be muleys about, so one tends to act like a mule deer hunter. A bigger mistake couldn't be made. THEY DON'T BEHAVE LIKE MULE DEER. There are only two ways to hunt. Number one, sit and glass, which I hate to do, but I spend a couple of hours each morning and night looking. Study every piece of possible concealment. They love to lay in the shade. A favorite location is at the base of a cactus. The only other way to kill your animal is to try and spook game out of potential hiding places. Rock throwing and slingshots seem to force bucks to their feet. The only problem is that most shots are on the run, which isn't very conducive to trophy judging. I have noticed that if there is a rain followed by a cold, dark night, deer are everywhere. This type of weather could be your chance."

During the same year, a mountable Columbia blacktail was added to the list. This 3 by 4 with an 18 inch-spread should be considered as an ex-

Jim Bush with Kodiak Island Sitka blacktail buck. Photo courtesy Jim Bush.

cellent trophy from northern California. For some strange reason, the season opens in August, which is much too early for quality hunting. It is usually closed long before the rut, but in 1983 an odd set of circumstances decreed that the rut would start before the deer season closed. Bucks seemed to be everywhere. Ed feels that the Columbian blacktail is the hardest of all to harvest for the head hunter.

He shares this bit of advice: "Killing a respectable Columbian blacktail buck is truly a difficult task. There aren't many out there and they live in very dense, heavy timber. This is still hunting at its finest. I probably move no more than one-half mile per hour. Once you jump a deer, it is still difficult to determine if it is what you want. Remember to hunt the edges early and late in the day. Stay away from California if you want to kill a big buck. The season is too early in the year when the bucks are difficult to find. California does allow the use of a single dog to chase deer from the brush. It works, but shots will be at running animals. How well can you judge a buck when it is running?"

Shoemaker with his 1985 southeast Alaska Sitka blacktail buck collected along a high ridge on Chichagof Island.

The year 1983 provided one more buck for Ed Shoemaker's trophy room, a 4 by 4 whitetail from the brush country of Texas. Rather than hunt in one of the traditional Texas styles, our hunter chose to still hunt. It proved to be effective as he saw 17 shootable bucks in only three days. Now he hopes to add a northern Montana whitetail to his collection this coming fall.

After applying for several years, Ed finally was lucky and drew an Arizona mule deer tag in an area famous for its quality hunting. Even though he harvested his best mule deer buck on this hunt, he feels that he only took a baby compared to what is available in some of Arizona's better trophy areas. His buck is a classy looking animal with a B&C score of 174, a 26-inch spread plus a high rack. He discovered that some units only have a few permits available, so a buck has good odds of living to an age needed to grow a trophy set of antlers. He noted that many nontypicals were being harvested with wide, heavy racks. They are a bit uneven and they don't have many extra points so they fail to score high. Nevertheless, they are beautiful trophies.

After completing his first Arizona muley hunt, along with visiting local hunters, he is convinced that he will eventually kill a high quality trophy.

The year 1985 yielded the final animal of Shoemaker's slam with a high country Sitka blacktail buck from Chichagof Island near Juneau, Alaska. Ed decided to stop and visit friends for a few days at Juneau after having completed a successful brown bear and mountain goat hunt with Jim Keeline of Yakutat, Alaska. Ed and his buddy, Dave Kemy, decided to try their hand at chasing alpine bucks. For those that think Coues' bucks have small antlers, they ain't seen nothing. A mere 100 B&C points earns a spot in the book and 108 points will place it in the all-time records. Compared to the 195 points it takes to get into the "Book" with a muley, a tiny Sitka head will be considered outstanding.

Hunting Alaska blacktails is generally tough work. The lower mountain slopes are covered with a jungle-like mixture of alders, willows, thorn-covered Devil's Club and salmon berry brush. In this environment, hiking time is measured in hours per mile. Once on top, the world unfolds into a scenic mixture of alpine plants and scattered ancient, twisting alpine hemlock trees. On a three-day hunt, Ed completed his slam with a forked horn buck. He now can hardly wait for a return trek to the high country of southeast Alaska and its diminutive bucks.

Before the coming of the heavy rainstorms of mid September, Alaska bucks tend to concentrate above timber line. Few hunters pursue the blacktail in the high habitats. They aren't particularly wary as they seldom see humans. After a few days of hard fall rains, the bucks are driven into the heavily forested midslopes and are almost impossible to find until winter's snows drive them to the beaches, late in December. One problem then is weather, which can keep you from going afield. Also, bucks will be shedding their antlers.

Alaska has deer on most of the coastal islands and part of the mainland between Ketchikan to the the south, then north and west to the Kodiak Island group. The latter area has been producing many good heads for the past decade. Alaska has a generous deer limit of up to five, with seasons often running from August 1 to December 31.

Ed Shoemaker's "slam" should be considered a true hunting accomplishment as he did it all without any guiding services.

When asked what suggestions he could pass on to others wishing to achieve similar goals, he gave the following advice: "I am constantly talking to others about hunting. When I hear something interesting, I follow up. If it takes long distance phone calls, that is the price of success. I always have questions for those with knowledge. Sporting magazines are a constant source of information. Much can be learned from them. Remember it takes research, and lots of it. There's a lot of bad advice out there, so you need to learn to sort it out."

When asked what his favorite deer rifle was, I was surprised to learn that he uses so many. His slam was collected with four different calibers:

A high scoring Afognak Island Sitka blacktail buck.

Columbia blacktail — 7X57 Mauser
Sitka blacktail — 300 Winchester Magnum
Coues' — 243 Winchester
Texas whitetail — 243 Winchester
Mule deer — 375 H&H

In addition, Shoemaker has killed deer with a 250/3000, a 30/06, a 30/30 and a 6mm. He says he has killed the most with a 30/06 and a 300 WM. The burro deer were all taken with the /06.

I asked what advice he could pass on to the new or young deer hunter? His answer was concise and valuable: "Spend lots of time deer hunting. Only by failure can we learn what is correct. Nothing beats time in the field. To collect trophies, hunt where it is genetically possible for big bucks, then spend time where the pressure is light. Even with favorable genes, it takes age to produce a big rack. Private property can be a plus. Recently, I have been trying to get permits where there is only a small number of deer tags issued, in areas where the gentic potential is good. Here, a buck can reach old age. There's big trophies out there for those willing to work."

Chapter Twenty

BEST ELK HUNT

Of all the big game trophy species in the world, perhaps the Rocky Mountain elk eludes the hunter's wall more than any other animal. I have talked with hunters who have been on 10 major, guided trips and have yet to kill a bull. Have you ever seen a picture of bull elk on their wintering grounds at Jackson Hole? Maybe there will be 50 or more bulls in the photo, and there won't be a single trophy head. In many areas that are heavily roaded, elk do not live long enough to grow antlers of significant size. I am told that in eastern Oregon few elk will ever live to an age to sport branched antlers.

What is a trophy elk? The definition will vary from hunter to hunter, but I think most knowledgeable hunters consider the minimum size to be a trophy is 300 B & C points, a 6 by 6 and boast a main beam approaching 50 inches in length. An elk with these dimensions, or larger, makes a mighty impressive mount. Why is it so hard to collect such an animal? Any elk is a difficult to harvest! In Montana, fewer than 13 percent of the licensed hunters kill an elk. Let's work from there.

Gary Wolfe, formerly of the Vermejo Park Corp., conducted a study entitled "The Relationship Between Age And Antler Development In Wapiti." Out of 480 harvested bulls in an area noted for its quality elk, only 10 percent scored 300 B & C points or greater. Not a single one came close to making the 375 minimum needed for the BOOK. Almost all trophy heads came from animals that were at least 7 1/2 years of age. It thus is obvious that an elk must have a chance of reaching old age before he can sport trophy headgear. By comparison, I have seen tremendous antlers on 4 1/2 year old mule deer. A lot of wild, unhunted country or a closely controlled harvest are prerequisites to trophy antler development.

To make matters worse, some areas do not seem to produce large antlers. In all sad stories we can find some ray of hope — even to the hunter's chances of killing a trophy bull elk. Even though in Montana only 13 percent of the hunters score on an elk, some years 75- 85 percent will kill on the post-season hunts — and all during a two or a four day period.

We moved to Montana on a permanent basis early in 1976. Jack Atcheson introduced me to one of his good friends, Kerry Constan, who is a game biologist for the state of Montana. He soon invited me to Lewistown for a hunt. I was most impressed with a few of his trophy heads, especially one set of elk antlers. After quizzing him a bit, he volunteered to share a few secrets. Here's what he had to say: "You know, Dunc, shooting a trophy elk has to be about the toughest goal that a big game hunter can set for himself. There is one bright note, however — the late season hunts north and west of Yellowstone National Park. This is not the old firing line that you have read about. It can be a quality experience. The one problem with the hunt is that they only give you a two day hunting period, as the state gets a high harvest even during such a short hunt. All they look at is the number harvested. IN MY OPINION, THE TROPHY ELK HUNTER WILL HAVE AS GOOD A CHANCE OF KILLING A LARGE BULL THEN AS HE WOULD DURING 20 YEARS OF HUNTING DURING THE REGULAR SEASON."

This last statement made during the fall of 1976 left a lasting impression on me. At the time there were 1,600 either-sex permits available on a drawing basis, with about one chance in two and a half of obtaining a tag. Not bad odds! During this era, about half the years provided excellent trophy hunting and half were a bust. The elk population was so high within the park that many biologists were fearing a massive die-off.

Initially there were plenty of large bulls to go around. Many outfitters were encouraging and almost insisting that their clients shoot an old bull even though the hunter might have been happier with a fine-tasting cow. With such pressure, the number of huge bulls had to diminish. In 1980-81, the state added 800 antlerless permits to the pot. Finally, for the 1983-84 season the state switched the quotas to 1,600 antlerless and 800 either-sex, with a maximum of 150 sportsmen afield at any one time. About 100 hunters checked in during each hunt period. Each week there was a Friday-Saturday hunt and a Sunday-Monday hunt, followed by a three-day rest period. In a letter to the author, Arnold J. Foss, State of Montana Regional Wildlife Manager, had the following to say about hunts in areas 310 and 313: "The overall effects of the hunting outside the park (1976-present) has resulted in some regulation of the herd segment that moves outside the park. The most recent estimate that the Park Service has for the Northern Yellowstone population is 16,000. We consider this a conservative figure. Only a small portion of the entire elk population actually moves outside the park. From 3,000 to 5,000 is a reasonable

Six by seven bull elk at the National Bison Range at Moiese, Montana. Photo by Allen D'Aigneau.

estimate, depending on the winter's severity. Our seasons only influence the population segment that is available to hunting. We have come close to keeping that segment in check, but it is very difficult to manage a portion of the population that has a variety of movement options. You will be able to see from the data summary below that we can anticipate some dry years with late hunts if the elk do not move. Because of the complexity of this situation, and the inability of our department to deal with the entire population, we have recognized that we can deal only with the animals that move outside. We have attempted to run an orderly hunt, keeping people numbers at reasonable levels for safety reasons and to try to maintain some element of quality in the hunt. I do not feel we have done too badly to date. However, we should clearly keep in mind that things will change over time and what appears to be a good system at this time may not be 10 years from now.

"We have influenced the reproduction performance of the population segment we are hunting. Cow-calf ratios are appreciably higher in the segment that is hunted regularly than is true in segments that are year-round inhabitants of the park.

"We have altered the sex structure of the segment that moves outside also. Since there were a lot of bulls available during the first hunts, more hunters selected bulls. We could see this coming but initially had little concern because we did not anticipate that elk would be available on an annual basis. The past three hunting seasons have provided at least an indication that movement may be more consistent than we have experienc-

The game pole at Point of Rocks Lodge during a late season hunt. The middle bull was green scored by the author at 380 B&C points and was taken by Max Chase, one of the great elk guides of Montana.

ed in past years, probably a function of high elk numbers. In view of this more consistent movement and hunter selection of bulls, the adjustment of permits (in terms of either-sex and antlerless categories) seemed appropriate. The structure for 1984-85 will reduce bull hunting to even a greater degree than in 1983-84.

If you compare the composition of bulls in the harvest from 1976 to 1983, you will see a reduction of about 50 percent. Part of this is due to the regulations we imposed, but the availability of bulls would be much less in later years.

"A summary of harvest information from the late Yellowstone seasons from 1976 through the 1983-84 hunting season is shown on page 163.

LATE SEASON ELK HARVEST
UNIT 313

Season Dates	Hunters	Bulls	Cows	Calves	Total	Hunter Success
1/9 – 3/1/76	1283	651	347	122	1120	87%
No Season 77	Flights indicated very little elk movement outside the Park.					
2/1 – 2/20/78	937	359	226	179	764	82%
2/1 – 2/20/79	Depradation hunt in the Slip and Slide – Sixmile Creeks area. It was estimated that approximately half of the 300 permit holders showed up and that they took about 70 elk.					
12/14/79–2/18/80	643	285	157	25	467	73%
	4 day hunting periods entire season.					
12/12/80–2/16/81	1109	71	40	15	126	11%
	4 day hunting periods Dec; 2 day periods the remainder of the season.					
12/11/81–2/15/82	1457	491	421	100	1012	70%
	4 day hunting periods Dec; 2 day periods the remainder of the season.					
12/10/82–2/14/83	1737	456	673	224	1353	78%
	4 day hunting periods Dec; 2 day periods the remainder of the season.					
12/9/83–2/13/84	1799	374	795	381	1550	86%
	4 day hunting periods Dec; 2 day periods the remainder of the season.					

Ten Year Summary of Age Structure of Elk Taken During The Gallatin Late Hunts From 1972 Through 1981

UNIT 310
Male

Year	1/2	1 1/2	2 1/2	3 1/2	Adults	8+	Total
1980–81	5	19	11	5	29	3	72
1979–80	32	22	16	4	14	2	90
1978–79	13	27	9	6	46	8	109
1977–78 [1]	7	22	14	1	35	1	80
1977–78 [2]	5	9	5	0	16	0	35
1976–77	0	0	4	3	5	0	12
1975–76	Not Held						
1974–75	26	33	21	0	43	0	123
1973–74	45	75	25	6	69	6	226
1972–73	48	39	22		58 [3]		167
1971–72	25	20	24		23 [4]	0	92
Totals	206	266	151	(25) [5]	(338)	(20)	1006

[1] Gallatin Hunt
[2] Madison phase of Gallatin hunt
[3] Includes 3 1/2 year olds and 8+ animals
[4] Includes 3 1/2 year olds but not 8+ animals
[5] Numbers in parenthesis indicate relative sample sizes but because of incomplete data summaries in 1972 and 1973, 3 1/2 and 8+ age classes are incompletely represented.

"One of the basic problems of age determination is getting an appropriate look at the teeth. If we can collect a jaw and compare it to known-age jaws, one can quite accurately assign an age class at least up to eight years of age. Under typical check station conditions, this is quite difficult. Most hunters with a nice bull are not too interested in someone removing jaws, etc. The data for the Gallatin area shows some variation in the portion of adult bulls from year to year, but a fairly consistent trend over the ten year period. It is apparent that few bulls over eight years of age are taken."

The 1987-88 plan for unit 313 is to issue 200 either-sex permits good for four hunting days, plus 1,800 antlerless permits, good for two days. It is now almost as difficult to draw an either-sex post season elk tag as a sheep or goat permit. In 1985-86, the drawing odds for either-sex 313 permits were one chance in 24. From what I saw for several seasons, this reduction in bull hunting was needed if we are to maintain any number of truly large bull elk. During these winters, I spent some time photographing wildlife within Yellowstone Park, near the north entrance at Gardiner. Until the winter of 1985-86, I did not see a single bull that would score 300 B&C points even though there were plenty of elk. This past winter I photographed several large bulls in the 375 point category. On a 1973 hunt to the Gardiner area, just before Thanksgiving, I spent part of a day in the same section of the park. I saw many bulls on that trip that would approach record book size. Let us be thankful that the Montana Department of Fish, Wildlife and Parks is trying to restore trophy bulls.

I drew my first late season tag for February 7-8, 1978. I was advised to book a guide for the two-day hunt, so as to make the most efficient use of my time. Information had it that there were several excellent outfitters, but I finally decided on Max Chase of Emigrant. He is the owner of Point of Rocks Lodge. At the time the cost of the two-day guided hunt, plus one extra day with room and board, was only $250. I soon found that I had made a wise choice in booking with Max.

Over a glass of scotch the night before the hunt, Max provided some insight into the late season hunts and his operation in particular. Max began: "A lot of hunters don't understand why the elk migrate to this area. This valley is very windy and the hillsides are generally blown free of snow, while the country within the park may be cursed with several feet of snow. It is the bulls that trigger the migration and it doesn't take that much snow to get them moving. We hunt mostly across the road from the lodge and that is about as far downriver as the herd travels. A high percentage of the elk that I hunt are big bulls. Maybe I will have 150 bulls within my hunting area at one time. Some people think I am killing too many resident bulls, but that is bunk. In any one year some of the park elk will not return to the safety of Yellowstone. They become new resident elk."

Long before dawn, we climbed aboard our horses and were off for the high country. A thousand feet above the highway the ground was still free of snow. As dawn's light illuminated the landscape, we could see mule deer scurrying about. They paid scant attention to us. Thirty minutes later we still had not seen an elk. I began to wonder — is Max was as good as his reputation?" I shouldn't have worried.

The areas open to hunting were small and I could see the boundary of our unit in the near distance. Snow began to accumulate. Within a quarter mile, we went from a few inches to three feet. Max motioned to dismount. Ahead lay an open hillside. He knew that there should be game feeding on the exposed vegetation. Suddenly, elk exploded from the grassy slope; all bulls. Max yelled, "Shoot." Five mature elk trotted within 100 yards of us. I decided that none were of true trophy size, so I held my fire. At the summit I could see a magnificent animal walk over the crest and stop, leaving his head, neck and antlers in view. He was a full 500 yards away. There were at least 40 head on the hill — all branch antlered bulls, with four sporting trophy-sized antlers. Suddenly a large 6 by 6 broke into the open, at 300 yards. I made my decision. I would take him rather than risk the chancy 500-yard shot at the larger bull. Later, my guide said that the boomer I passed up would have surely sported 60-inch main beams and that he was a regal 7 by 7, a potential "Book" head.

For my first shot I dropped to the snow and fired from the prone position with my 270. The bull faltered. I quickly fired my second and final shot. A trophy bull elk lay on the snow. A glance at my watch said it was 9 a.m. His 6 by 6 antlers later measured 52 4/8 inches on the main beam, with a 42 inch inside spread and a B & C score of 322 2/8 points. Four and one half years later he scored 259 5/8 by the Safari Club method. As

A 6 by 5 bull elk shot by the author on a late season Unit 313 hunt in Montana.

The author's best bull elk, which he collected on a late season Unit 313 hunt with Max Chase as guide.

is typical of Yellowstone elk, he has poor brow and fifth points. Today, his head adorns the place of honor on one wall of my combination North American trophy room/bedroom.

I was not lucky in the drawing again until four years later when I obtained a tag for January 15-16. Once again I booked a hunt with Max Chase. The weekend before my hunt one of my neighbors, Don Jensen, hunted with Max and collected a most outstanding head that I am certain would score in the 350 B & C point range. I arrived two days early to scout and photograph big game. Max had three hunters besides me to guide. One of them was Kerry Constan, the biologist, who originally advised me to draw for a unit 313 tag.

The weather the day before my hunt was miserable, with minus zero temperatures combined with strong winds — hardly enjoyable conditions. With the aid of my spotting scope, I saw over a dozen trophy bulls. With any luck at all, I knew that I should score on another fine trophy. That night we listened to the weather forecast. The first day of my hunt would be blessed with subzero temperatures, winds of 20-30 m.p.h. combined with a snow storm. The forecast for the next day was worse. That night I tossed and turned and tried to make a decision. "Should I hold out for a 6 by 6?" With my large family to feed the meat was very important, but I had been waiting for four years to receive this coveted permit. What should I do? About the time Max turned on my light at 4 a.m., I had made my decision. If the weather proved to be as bad as predicted I would shoot the first 5 by 5, or larger, that I saw.

Max decided that we would ride from the lodge instead of trucking the horses part way. This meant we would have a cold two-hour, pre-dawn ride. Before reaching the summit we split, each of us with our own guide. As the first rays of light started to break somewhere below the horizon I recognized the hill where the other bull had been shot. Suddenly we could see elk in two directions. We dropped from our horses and sneaked in for a closer look. At 350 yards we could see that there was one branch antlered bull with the herd. He shouldn't have been with cows at this time of year, but there he was. I decided to risk the long shot from the sitting position rather than try and sneak closer, and maybe end up with a running 200 yard shot. I held for the lungs and fired. The bull ran and my second was on its way. Later it was found that both were solid hits. A half hour later, after several more shots, I had a 6 by 5 bull laying at my feet. He had so-so 43-inch beams and a 39-inch spread — not a bad elk but not a trophy.

Thirty minutes later I was a happy man for we were dragging my animal through a raging, blinding snowstorm. My decision had been wise. I have seldom seen it snow with this intense fury, at such a low temperature (-4 degrees F). Once again I had scored at 9 a.m.

We were back at the lodge with my bull long before noon. I did not head towards Missoula, however, as the state had closed the Interstate highway leading west and home.

A few days before my arrival at Point of Rocks Lodge, Max had collected a high scoring bull for himself. I rough-measured this tremendous 8 by 7 elk at 380 points — a trophy of a lifetime by any standard. This was Max's second record book bull that I know of.

In 1983 I did not draw a tag, but my friend John Farley had secured an antlerless permit. Jim Olsen and I accompanied John on his hunt. Hunting from the road, my friend scored within minutes on a fine-eating cow.

The following winter my wife, Pat, was lucky enough to draw a cow tag. She had never killed an elk, so we decided to see what she could collect. At first light we found that we were sharing a herd of elk with several other hunters. Pat dropped one, which she lost, as some other hunter ran to it and put his tag on the animal. Fifteen minutes later, Pat had another elk on the ground. At the check station we found that well over 80 percent of the hunters were scoring, but mostly on cows. Not many hunters were killing old bulls.

Now that we are into 1987, Montana is continuing a policy of restricted either-sex elk hunting during the late season hunts. During the winter of 1986-87, there were 4,458 first choice applicants for 200 unit 313 late season, either-sex elk tags, or only about one person in 22 drew a tag. Not too good. The odds were much better for those that would settle for an antlerless permit with 4,685 listing the 313 hunt as first choice for 1,800 licenses.

I just returned (December 1986) from a photography trip to the Gardiner area. I am happy to report that I saw many trophy bulls. They seem to be coming back. Hopefully, this soon will again be the "Best Elk Hunt."

Chapter Twenty-one

MONTANA THE GREAT LAND

One afternoon late in January of 1976, as I was plowing the yard of our Afognak Island logging camp, I saw my partner, Cliff Reeves, walking towards me from a Grumman Widgeon that had just landed. I shut the tractor off as he approached. Cliff's first words were, "Dunc, think you could book any bear hunters for this spring?" I knew what was coming; my partners wanted to buy my interest in Afognak Logging Inc.

Later that evening over a toddy, Pat and I told our friends at camp that it looked like we would be leaving. Surprisingly, several people told us that we should look at the Bitterroot Valley in western Montana as a site for our new home. I had traveled south to Montana several times to hunt in the fall. We had always thought that maybe, someday, when I was 50 or so, we would move to the Big Sky State, but surely not at the tender, young age of 40. Pat surprised me with her thoughts. "Dunc, you always talk so much about Montana. Why don't you go down there and take a look around. If you like what you see, buy a place. As long as I can get to church, I will be happy."

The next morning when leaving for the Lower 48 I had three places to inspect: two in Idaho and the Bitterroot Valley. After reaching Hamilton, Montana, I never made it to Idaho. Hamilton is a clean, modern western Montana town with a climate that can't be beat in the Rockies. I reasoned with my limited amount of personal knowledge that I would live in Montana. As a serious sportsman one would have tremendous opportunities as a resident. Nonresidents only get a limited chance in the big game tag drawings in Montana. Wyoming treats the nonresident so well, he may have just as good a chance to receive a tag as a resident. In Idaho there are so few drawing tags that no one has much of a chance. When one lives so close to Idaho as does the resident of the Bitterroot, it is about as easy to hunt in Idaho as in Montana. Without a question, Montana has to be the greatest state in the Rockies for the fisherman. At the time, I wanted to live close to the Canadian border, in order to easily fly my Cub to Alaska.

After two days of looking, I signed a purchase offer on a four bedroom house overlooking the valley. If a person travels one mile west of my home he can drive a vehicle no further in that direction. From there it is 70 miles westward across the Selway-Bitterroot Wilderness to the next road, and I mean any road. From my front door it is only a couple of miles to a national forest trailhead where one can hunt elk, mule deer, whitetail, black bear, mountain goat and moose. In less than 10 minutes I can walk to a trout stream where I can catch pansized brookies and cutthroats. To the east, I can drive on a paved road for two miles and reach the famed Bitterroot River, where I can fish for whitefish, rainbows, dollies, brookies, cutthroats and brown trout. One evening in 20 minutes I caught four trout — a brookie, a cut, a rainbow and a brown trout.

When first moving to the Bitterroot I knew I had picked a good place to live, but really didn't know how good. After a year, or so, I began to think of moving again to Dillon or Lewistown, Montana, or maybe Cody, Wyoming. Today I am convinced we are living where we should. As a bonus after the Montana hunter gets all the many deer tags that are available, the Bitterroot archer can buy five more whitetail tags for the riverbottom. Some years the riverbottom season is six months long.

In a half day's drive a person can reach Glacier National Park or add a couple more hours and one can travel to Yellowstone. In less than two hours I can drive to the Moiese National Bison Range to photograph bison, antelope, mule deer, whitetails, elk, bighorns and mountain goats. Within three hours a fisherman can reach a gallery of trout waters that sound like the "who's who" of trout. I often travel to the Big Hole for an evening of fly casting. This river is rated by many as the top dryfly fishing river in the United States. This scenic body of water is the only river in the Lower 48 with native grayling. One evening during a particularly good hatch I had strikes, on dry flies, on 40 consecutive casts. After the 40th I quit and went home. Not even in Alaska is fishing often quite that good. My record in Alaska is 17 fish on 17 casts. Last fall near Yakutat I did about that well fishing for silver salmon. A lake that is only a three-hour drive from my home boasts rainbows and browns of a huge size. My friend Glenn, in a good month, may land 75 trout over three pounds from this one water. One day he landed two 12-pound browns. Two weeks ago a man gave me a 4 3/4 pound eastern brook trout to mount that was caught just a few miles from my house.

On the whole, I see more game in Montana than in Alaska, with the exception of choice deer and caribou locations. In central and eastern Mon-

One of the reasons Montana offers such great hunting is terrain that varies from open grasslands to timbered draws, forested mountain slopes and true alpine country..

tana, deer and antelope herds have recently enjoyed peak numbers. It is common to see 300 deer in a day, and a hundred is just so-so. According to my diary, during the past five seasons I have seen an average of one and a half mature 5 by 5's per day. One morning last fall we saw 15 5 by 5's, including several mounters. In the mountainous western part of the state one will not see large numbers of muleys, but here is where one might find a real buster. In 1983. a foreign hunter shot a monster typical muley, near my home that measured green 217 6/8 B & C points, with a 37 1/2 inch spread. It may never be officially scored scored as it has left the United States. This past fall (1986) in some units, an antelope hunter was allowed to harvest up to three extra animals, but they had to be does.

On the subject of record book heads, for the past several years Montana has dominated new B & C bighorn entries. In 1984 alone, it produced 10 new rams that scored over the minimum. One unit with a quota of 10 produced six over the minimum, including one of the largest rams to ever be killed from this state. In 1985 the number increased to 12 or 13. One unit in our valley is producing 3/4 curl rams with 15 inch bases in just 2 1/2 years. I saw one 4 1/2 year old ram that was killed from this unit last season that boasted 37-inch plus horns. Compare this growth with an average of seven years to reach 3/4 curl in the Brooks Range. Montana has been following an active program of bighorn transplanting in recent years. We have so many surplus sheep that we now even harvest a con-

Fred Mercer killed the number four elk in 1957 in southwestern Montana. This tremendous head scores 419 4/8 B&C points.

siderable number of ewes each year. Pat and my boys apply for a ewe tag every year and one will draw a permit most every season. The meat is of top quality.

About 25 percent of the elk listed in the Boone and Crookett Record Book come from Montana, which is more than any other two states combined. The number four elk killed by Fred Mercer was taken in the Gravelly Mountains of southwestern Montana. The Fish and Game Department feels that pressure is starting to be excessive in some areas, if we are to maintain quality trophy elk hunting in our state. It takes about seven years to grow a big bull. In areas like eastern Oregon it is difficult to find any branch antlered bulls. Our game commission is starting to think in terms of trophy management.

Some 10 percent of the bulls harvested in Montana are 6 by 6's or larger. If you can draw an either-sex post season tag in unit 313 or 310, your chance of taking a big bull elk are excellent. I have received two such tags and have killed a moderate-sized 6 by 5 and a big 6 by 6 that scored 322 plus.

The author owns this nontypical muley rack that scores an unofficial 248-plus B&C points.

Montana is also the only state south of Canada where the sportsman can still hunt the grizzly bear. The quota has been 25 per year killed by any cause, but was considerably reduced to 15 this past year. Antihunting groups have recently tried to protest this season, so the state published an environmental impact statement. In the preliminary draft the experts stated that some habitats have enough grizzlies that they may soon be delisted to threatened. When I was researching for my book *On Bears And Bear Hunting*, I found that seasonally some habitats may have as many as one grizzly per square mile, which ranks with high density brown bear country in Alaska.

Montana is also the only state that has an unlimited number of permits available for bighorn rams in some units. They are hard to find, but the good hunters score. Nearly all of Jack Atcheson Jr.'s clients earn at least shot at a ram.

Montana's antelope hunting has to be in a class by itself, possibly only equalled in Wyoming. If one applies in the right unit you can draw a tag every year, which in some areas is good for two or more animals. I often see hundreds of animals in a single day. Two years ago one client missed over 40 shots at standing antelope during a three-day period before scoring. These shots ran from 75 to 300 yards and most were taken from a rest. You could hardly get more opportunities than this in Africa. All shots were fired at bucks with at least a 12-inch horn.

Two years ago, between my wife and me, plus two sons, we put 20 big game animals in the freezer. Last year because of some selective trophy hunting the number dropped to 13. This year we took 16. We have all this fun plus we live in a nice area with good people as neighbors. Our average annual precipitation is 11.96 inches. In 10 years I have never seen over 10 inches of snow on the ground at one time. During the winter it seldom drops to below zero and yet 50 miles away it may be 40 degrees colder. In the summer it will only rise to above 95 once every few years, and it always cools off at night. Air conditioners are a rarity in this valley.

When I give lectures on hunting, people often ask how I ever managed to leave such a wonderful place as Alaska. I just look back and smile.

Duncan Gilchrist standing by his plane. He has more than 6,000 hours as a bush pilot.

Chapter Twenty-two

NOW LET'S GO HUNTING

Now that you have read this book, you should be prepared to head to the field, ready to hunt. I never claim to know all the answers, or that my system will lead you along the only trail to success. However, my methods do work and will bring success if faithfully followed.

Throughout the text, I have referred to others who are considered as superior hunters. It should be noted that each of these sportsmen often uses a different system, and yet each gets the job done. One common factor with all successful hunters is their dedication to hunt as hard as possible. Each learns all he can about his quarry before fine tuning individual hunting techniques. All expect success and will not accept failure. They are the 10 percenters of the hunting world.

I have been reading hunting books since I was a young child and have read through many a page to glean a single, helpful suggestion. The search for helpful information can be most frustrating to the enthusiastic student of big game hunting. Thus was born the series of short courses presented in this book. Each chapter attempts to give as much knowledge to the hunter as possible, in a minimum of words. The beginning hunter should achieve success if he follows the concepts to their limit. The more advanced sportsman should garner scattered bits that may make the difference between success or failure.

While talking to others on how to hunt the various species, I have been exposed to many new thoughts and methods. These interviews are going to make me a better hunter too. As an example, in "Short Course on Elk Hunting", I consulted with Jack Atcheson, Dale Burk and Larry Hilton, all highly successful elk hunters. Each consistently scores on quality elk, and yet each uses an entirely different method. One should never lose sight of the fact that each man is a master of his own system.

Within each of the "Some Thoughts on... " chapters, I have attempted to convey ideas which will help you become a more accomplished sportsman. This series of chapters tells how I get the job done. You may have equally as good, or better methods, but my way will also work.

I never claim to be the best hunter in the world, but I have enjoyed life in the back country and have experienced hunting in some of the finest game fields of the world. All my adventures have been on a very modest budget, while supporting a family of eight. I am both a trophy and a meat hunter, out of necessity. Average representative male animals satisfy my desires, but because of good luck, some have been top trophies — luck that I pulled the trigger on an extra large male rather than a so-so animal. The consistent taking of game is not luck. It is the application of well-applied techniques. The man that always scores never gives up. More game is shot during the last hour of a hunt than ever was during the first day. Motivation is important in hunting, as with so many endeavors. A hunter needs to define his goals — and they should be written and referred to at a later date. A superior hunter then will realize that he makes his own luck.

When in the field, enjoy it all — the comaraderie, the camping, the scenery, the experience itself, as well as collecting an animal. Some animals come easy, others with great difficulty, and a few don't seem to fall to the rifle at all. Each trip afield shall be remembered as an experience in itself.